THE DESPERATE DIPLOMAT

THE DESPERATE DIPLOMAT

SABURO KURUSU'S MEMOIR OF THE WEEKS BEFORE PEARL HARBOR

EDITED BY

J. Garry Clifford and Masako R. Okura

UNIVERSITY OF MISSOURI PRESS   COLUMBIA

University of Missouri Press, Columbia, Missouri 65211
Printed and bound in the United States of America

First paperback printing, 2019.

ISBN: 978-0-8262-2037-0 (hardcover : alk. paper)
ISBN: 978-0-8262-2201-5 (paperback : alk. paper)

Library of Congress Control Number: 2015940587

♾™ This paper meets the requirements of the American National Standard for Permanence of Paper for Printed Library Materials, Z39.48, 1984.

Typeface: Minion Pro

Contents

The Inside Story of the Japanese-American Negotiation: Our Diplomatic History

by Saburo Kurusu

THE DESPERATE DIPLOMAT

Foreword

"It is so gratifying that the passage of time has allowed my father's diplomatic endeavors to be viewed with greater objectivity and accuracy." —Pia Kurusu White

My great-grandmother's stories of her experiences growing up have amazed and intrigued me from a young age. She has been immersed in many different cultures of the world and has experienced both living with royalty and surviving without heat and food during war. My great-grandmother—or Nana, as we call her—grew up around some of the most prominent figures in recent history and received an education greater than any level of schooling could offer. The events in her life are something I could not imagine in my wildest dreams.

Many times, children of diplomats are absent from their parent's career and life due to constant travel and such demanding jobs. For Nana, this was not the case. Her father, Special Envoy Saburo Kurusu, took his children with him every chance he had and was a very loving and present figure in their lives. He was largely responsible for my grandmother's extraordinary childhood. Although I never met him, I feel that through Nana sharing her experiences, I have an understanding of the caring and remarkable man that he was.

Here is a small glimpse at the life of Saburo Kurusu through my great-grandmother's words:

> "Although we were aware of the importance of his career, to us he was always the very affectionate Papa, as we called him. My father was determined to be a loving and affectionate parent because he did not receive that from his own father. After returning home from his first diplomatic post, my father was not greeted by his father but only by the family driver. He searched excitedly through the house to finally find his father reading a newspaper in the study. His father

lowered the paper from his eyes to say hello and then never spoke to him again. My mother speculated that the reason for the cold reception my father got was because my grandfather was displeased when his favorite son did not follow in his own footsteps: My grandfather founded and ran a ship-building company. Ironically, accompanying his father to business meetings with people from other countries may have been what influenced my father's decision to enter the foreign service. Needless to say, after this encounter, my father was convinced that when he had children, he would have a much more loving and warm relationship with them.

"Father was brought up in a household of seven siblings: four brothers and three sisters. Due to my grandmother's obsession with cleanliness and order in her house, all the children lived in a separate house on the property, with nannies to care for them, and they were only allowed in the main house to visit the parents once a day in the evening. Grandfather, however, became attached to my father and his younger sister and took them frequently on business trips to meet with foreign customers. My aunt recounted their excitement at staying in western-style hotels, sleeping on beds instead of futons on the floor, and eating foods which seemed exotic to them.

"I think that perhaps my father's greatest asset to his career was my mother. She was unfailingly loyal and a superbly capable diplomat herself. As my father once told me, she would give the most intelligent and insightful advice when he sought it. They met when my father was on a post in New York. He was charged to accompany a delegation of farmers from Japan to the A&P Warehouse facility. Their guide happened to be my mother's older brother, who was employed as a refrigeration engineer. Uncle Norman was so intrigued with his first meeting with a Japanese man who spoke perfect English that he invited my father to dinner at my grandmother's house. My mother was also present at the dinner, and, as they say, the rest was history.

"My father was posted to Chicago shortly after their marriage. There, my sister Jaye and brother Ryo were born. I was a Johnny-come-lately when my father was first secretary at the Japanese embassy in Rome in 1926.

"My fond recollection of my father was his compassionate and gentle nature. My mother was our disciplinarian, but my father would always give everyone the benefit of the doubt regarding any misdeeds. It was my father's routine to recline on the chaise longue in the bedroom after breakfast to peruse all the daily newspapers, with our dog Jimmy snoozing on his tummy. One day, my father quickly lowered the newspaper to speak to my mother, and the dog jumped up and nipped him on the nose. My mother immediately started to swat Jimmy with a paper, but my father kept saying, "Don't hurt him. He only naturally reacted to my sudden move." If he treated even our pets with this much love and forgiveness, it is no wonder he was so affectionate with us, his children.

"I believe it was at about ten years of age that I began to fully understand and appreciate my father as a dedicated professional. Until then, he was just Papa, who always generously shared his free time with us.

World affairs and my father's views, when shared with us, became a source of invaluable education and interest. With this knowledge of my father's character and beliefs, the negative public reaction created subsequent to my father's greatest diplomatic challenge and effort, to attain peace between Japan and the United States, was unthinkable and hurtful. I remember that my father felt very distressed that he was unsuccessful in the negotiation, and he undoubtedly indulged in thinking of many what-ifs.

"Right after the war, I was working as a liaison officer between the prefectural government and the American occupation forces. There was an American officer I had to deal with who was so rude and demanding that he made my job unpleasant. One day, at the dinner table, I went on and on about this man and immediately incurred my father's rebuke. Shocked at having been subjected to my father's severe criticism for the first time in my life, I ran from the table in tears. My father followed me and hugged me without a word, and all was well again. My mother later told me that if I ever played the drama queen and upset my father again, I could kiss my happy home good-bye!

"Due to the way my father was portrayed in the states, my parents had concerns for the reception my sister and I would encounter upon our arrival in the U.S. as brides of American men. My mother even wrote a touching letter to my in-laws recounting the kind welcome she had received from my father's family upon her arrival in Japan, and she prayed they would find it in their hearts to reciprocate in the same way. My parents' concerns turned out to be groundless, as both of us encountered nothing but kindness and acceptance.

"Even through the seriousness of his profession, my father always kept his easygoing personality and sense of humor through to his retirement. He and his friend [Mr. Yoshida]who was ambassador to the Court of St. James and later became the postwar prime minister, loved going to the zoo when my father visited England. They would go to watch the monkeys and pick out ones who reminded them of

> people they knew. This peculiar pastime stands out in my memory because when I think of him, the first thing that comes to mind is not his profession, his many diplomatic successes, or his failures. When I think of my father, I am reminded of his warm and uplifting personality that was evident to everyone he met."

I am very grateful that careful research and time has been put into print to allow readers the opportunity to view my great-great-grandfather's diplomatic endeavors regarding relations with Japan and the United States during World War II with proper accuracy. My wish is that when readers have completed this book, the true memory of Saburo Kurusu will change the hearts of all who are misinformed.

Ashley A. White
Great-great-granddaughter of Saburo Kurusu
Student at the University of Michigan

Pia Kurusu White
Daughter of Saburo Kurusu
Amazing wife, mother, grandmother, friend, teacher, and student

Preface and Acknowledgments

It is often said that history is written by the winners. For Americans, the history surrounding the events of December 7, 1941—"a date which will live in infamy"—will always be controversial. Countless books and articles have attempted to explain why the U.S. Navy's Pacific Fleet was caught so unprepared on that fateful Sunday morning in Hawaii. Iconic movies about Japan's surprise attack like *Tora! Tora! Tora!* (1970) are etched in our collective memory. For many, it remains a story of heroes and villains. Even though historians have tried to correct misperceptions and puncture stereotypes, one individual has stood out as the apparent embodiment of Japanese treachery in 1941: Saburo Kurusu, Japan's special envoy who flew across the Pacific to participate in eleventh-hour diplomatic negotiations, has been cast as the archvillain in the historic melodrama. Unlike Japan's official ambassador, Kichisaburo Nomura, a retired admiral who had made many friends in Washington, DC, Kurusu was viewed with distrust from the outset. That Kurusu, as Japan's ambassador to Germany, had signed the Tripartite Pact with Germany and Italy in September 1940 helps explain the skepticism. Access to Japanese diplomatic communications through intercepts by the Magic cryptanalysis project's also led some U.S. officials to think—mistakenly—that Kurusu might be privy to Tokyo's military plans, because some cables mentioned imminent deadlines after which things would "automatically" happen. Such suspicion turned into near certainty after Pearl Harbor as Americans searched for scapegoats. Even First Lady Eleanor Roosevelt could refer to Kurusu as that "nasty little Jap" who had distracted her husband while Japanese planes bombed Manila and Honolulu.

If Americans had looked more closely, however, they might have seen the smiling, bespectacled diplomat in a much different light. Because his wife did not come with him to Washington in 1941, most observers did not know that Kurusu had married an American, Alice Jay Little, when he was a consular official in Chicago in 1914. It was a most successful marriage, with the gracious Alice Kurusu accompanying her husband to a succession of important posts in the 1920s and '30s—the Philippines, Chile, Peru, Greece, Italy, and two times to Germany. When Kurusu was appointed ambassador to Belgium in 1936, the Kurusus (by then the best-known couple among Japanese diplomats) not only became favorites of King Leopold III and the royal family but also befriended US ambassador Joseph E. Davies and his wife, Marjorie Merriweather Post. The famous newsreel images of Kurusu signing the Tripartite Pact in 1940 obscured the fact that he personally opposed the Axis alliance and particularly disliked German foreign minister Joachim Von Ribbentrop. That Adolf Hitler sent Alice Kurusu an enormous bouquet of red roses and Hermann Goering personally showed her the looted art treasures of his Karinhall estate did not mean that the Kurususes were in any way pro-Nazi. Indeed, Kurusu asked to be recalled as soon as he signed the Axis treaty. If officials in Washington had paid more attention to the favorable reports from Tokyo by Kurusu's good friend Ambassador Joseph Grew, they might have better understood that the special envoy who arrived at the eleventh hour ranked with Nomura, Shigenori Yoshide, Mamoru Shigemitsu, and other so-called moderates who wanted desperately to avoid war with the United States. They might have realized that Saburo Kurusu was the genuine peace-seeker he claimed to be.

In Kurusu's own English translation of his memoir, published herein, readers can understand and empathize with the diplomat's near-impossible mission in those dramatic weeks before Pearl Harbor. Faced with an increasingly tight deadline, negotiating with interlocutors he barely knew, burdened with instructions that could not be altered, frustrated by American rigidity after initial optimism, and lacking any knowledge of Japan's military plans, Kurusu strove valiantly to keep diplomacy going, to avert a war he knew would be catastrophic. Even after US secretary of state Cordell Hull rejected any temporary modus vivendi and issued his ten-point "ultimatum," Kurusu did not give up. With Nomura's concurrence, he disobeyed Tokyo's instructions by seeking help from the "side," as he put it, utilizing Davies, the Reverend E. Stanley Jones, and Bernard M. Baruch to suggest that President Franklin D. Roosevelt reopen the diplomatic dialogue by sending a peace message directly to Emperor Hirohito. Unfortunately, that cable arrived too late. Kurusu failed—but not for lack of effort.

Even in his sometimes circular English prose, his emotions and strong feelings come across vividly—his amazement and gratitude that Hirohito had worried about his health in approving his mission to Washington, his poignant farewell meeting with Grew at the US Embassy and his emotional hat-doffing gesture when he glimpsed Grew again at an African coastal port in 1942, and his great relief when, after Pearl Harbor, he learned that Baruch did not regard him as duplicitous. Despite Kurusu's regrets that he did not do more to prevent war in 1941 and despite his metaphor that treaties and agreements were akin to sketchings on the sand too easily washed away by the clash of national interests, what is most memorable in this memoir is Kurusu's persistent commitment to the art of diplomacy. He did not stop trying. "Working for peace is not as simple as starting a war," Kurusu told Premier Hideki Tōjō on his return to Japan in the summer of 1942. Those are words worth remembering.

Two internal grants from Columbus State University funded Masako Okura's research trip to Tokyo in June 2011, some three months after the Fukushima earthquake and tsunami had rocked Japan. With great assistance from archivists at the National Diet Library, she spent seven days leafing through materials in the Saburo Kurusu papers on the fourth floor—handwritten memos in both languages from the 1941 negotiations, portraits of his American wife, Alice, a letter from Grew, old newspaper articles, and the like. During this time, she came to feel closer to Kurusu. He was no longer an abstract figure in history, but a man who lived and breathed, and who agonized over his impossible burden of continuing diplomatic negotiations and averting a disastrous war. Amid sweltering temperatures, with air conditioners shut off to save energy, a book-length document in English caught her eye. Mostly typed but with handwritten comments and revisions, it turned out to be an English translation of Kurusu's second memoir, *Nichi-Bei Gaikō Hiwa*, published in 1952. The document had come to the library when the diplomat's Japanese family had donated his papers in 2007. The purpose of Kurusu's translation was not clarified by supporting documents in his papers; perhaps it was intended for his wife, who could speak Japanese fluently but read the language with difficulty, or possibly for his daughters, Jaye and Pia, both of whom had married Americans and moved to the United States. More likely, however, Kurusu intended to publish his book for an English-speaking readership to tell his side of the story and to refute the prevailing negative perceptions about him. His premature death in 1954 thwarted such a plan. It is only appropriate that we have undertaken to retell Kurusu's story sixty years later.

In editing Kurusu's memoir for publication, we have made occasional changes in punctuation, grammar, and wording, always checking such changes against the original Japanese to make certain that we did not alter his meaning. We also have done our best to provide the full names of the many individuals mentioned by Kurusu in his narrative, and we have modified the spelling of several place names in accordance with current usage (i.e., Macau instead of Macao; Mozambique rather than Zanzibar).

We wish to thank individuals who pointed us toward research materials, for commenting on earlier drafts of our book, and for other assistance: Michael Barnhart, John Chambers, Mike Chapman, Frank Costigliola, Taka Daitoku, Justus Doenecke, Greg P. Domin, Mike Donoghue, Susan Dunn, Bob Ferrell, Irv Gellman, Waldo Heinrichs, Peter Mauch, Bob Montgomery, Virginia Montgomery, George Nash, Kent Newmyer, Tom Paterson, Kurt Piehler, Mark Stoler, Brian Waddell, Ed Wehrle, Hal Wert, Ted Wilson, and Sherry Zane. We are grateful to the two anonymous peer reviewers for the University of Missouri Press for their helpful suggestions. Thanks, too, to Bob Clark and Matt Hanson at the Roosevelt Presidential Library for their last-minute efforts.

Lastly, with profound gratitude, we acknowledge the invaluable assistance of Pia Kurusu White and Ashley A. White, Saburo Kurusu's daughter and his great-great-granddaughter, respectively. Not only did they provide us with wonderful photographs of their father and family, but they also captured the generous spirit and warm personality of a dedicated diplomat who worked indefatigably for peace.

JGC & MRO

Introduction

The Pacific War had ended abruptly. Chief Allied prosecutor Joseph B. Keenan was interrogating veteran Japanese diplomat Saburo Kurusu in late 1945 in preparation for the forthcoming Tokyo War Crimes Trials. As the two men gazed out a large window overlooking the devastation of postwar Tokyo, Keenan remarked that it might take fifty years before Japan could fully recover from the war. Keenan then looked hard at Kurusu and said, "As far as the war is concerned, there is one name that ordinary Americans cannot forget. It is not [Foreign Minister Shigenori] Tōgō or [Prime Minister Hideki] Tōjō, but it is Kurusu."[1]

Keenan accurately characterized the prevailing American perceptions of the special envoy whom Tokyo had sent to Washington some three weeks before the Japanese attack on Pearl Harbor four years earlier.[2] In contrast to mild-mannered Ambassador Kichisaburo Nomura, a former admiral well respected by the Roosevelt administration, Kurusu—a smiling, small-statured career diplomat with a fluent command of English—was viewed with suspicion from the beginning. Racist assumptions partly accounted for such mistrust.[3] As Secretary of State Cordell Hull later noted in his memoirs, neither Kurusu's "appearance nor his attitude commanded confidence or respect" and that his purpose was "to lull us with talk until the moment Japan got ready to strike." His "only recommendation in my eyes was that he spoke excellent English, having married his American secretary."[4] Undersecretary of State Sumner Welles similarly disparaged Kurusu's "oily manner" and compared his allegedly deceitful role to that of "the goat tethered as bait for the tiger."[5] On the day of the Pearl Harbor bombing, even First Lady Eleanor Roosevelt complained about that "nasty little Jap [Kurusu] sitting there talking to my husband while Japanese planes were attacking Honolulu and Manila. And he was so nice to me when I came into the room to tell Franklin something. So polite and bowing and scraping."[6]

Average Americans also embraced the image of Kurusu as deceitful diplomat in the widely viewed 1943 film documentary *Prelude to War*, in which the narrator commented on Kurusu's signing of the Tripartite Pact with Germany and Italy in September 1940 by snidely calling him "our smiling little friend who later warmed his way into our hearts in December 1941."[7] Kurusu himself learned of his infamous reputation while interned after Pearl Harbor at the Homestead Hotel in Hot Springs, Virginia, where he encountered a giant graffiti that read, "I don't know who the hell Kurusu is but I want to hang him." Later, he became familiar with a new Americanism: Just as the name of Norway's Vidkun Quisling, who collaborated with the Nazis, had become synonymous with traitor, so too had the phrase "double Kurusu" come to mean "betrayal" or "double cross."[8] Indeed, a U.S. Senator on the Foreign Relations Committee demanded that "Ambassador Kurusu be thrown overboard in the Atlantic" when the diplomat was repatriated to Japan in the summer of 1942.[9]

The reality, however, differed from the reputation. As Kurusu himself told American reporters in 1945, he was "deeply hurt" by accusations that he had been "bait for the trap." He claimed—accurately—that he had not known about the planned attack on Pearl Harbor, that he had worked indefatigably for peace in 1941, and that the government in Tokyo could have "called off" the attack "at the very last minute" if he had succeeded in "maintaining peace."[10] Kurusu resented being called treacherous and double crossing by Americans. "I have worked hard for peace. Now, in this war, I have lost everything—my reputation, my home, my only son. Let no one think I like war."[11]

Prior to his death in 1954 at age sixty-eight, Kurusu published two diplomatic memoirs in which he explained and defended his extended efforts to stave off war in the last three weeks before Pearl Harbor.[12] These volumes have not been published in English. The one scholarly article on Kurusu in English, published in 1952, focuses on the special envoy's role in the abortive *modus vivendi* that was rejected by Secretary Hull on November 26, 1941.[13] The greater accessibility of Japanese diplomatic records for 1941 as well as recent biographies of Kurusu's colleagues Ambassador Nomura and Embassy First Secretary Hidenari Terasaki, not to mention the recent seventieth anniversary of the outbreak of the Pacific War, suggest that a reexamination of Kurusu's desperate diplomacy is long overdue.[14] This introduction will confirm that in sharp contrast to his duplicitous reputation, Kurusu, perhaps more than any other key player in the run-up to war in 1941, carried out what State Department official-turned-historian Herbert Feis has defined as "the first duty of a good diplomat—never to let peace fail because men grow weary of the hunt for tolerable terms."[15]

The origins of Kurusu's special mission are well known. Ambassador Nomura, a career naval officer whose clumsiness with both diplomatic protocol and spoken English was impeding his mission, had requested Kurusu's assistance earlier that summer.[16] This request in early August had come at a critical juncture following the German invasion of the Soviet Union in June and the subsequent occupation of southern Indochina by the Japanese in late July. The Roosevelt administration responded by freezing Japan's financial assets and embargoing oil exports to the island empire. Conversations continued over the next several months between Ambassador Nomura and Secretary Hull, but without success. Unless exports of American oil resumed, Japan was determined to seize the Dutch and British petroleum fields of Southeast Asia. "If we are going to fight," Japan's navy chief of staff informed Emperor Hirohito, "then the sooner . . . the better because our supplies are dwindling anyway."[17] But Washington would not turn on the oil spigot until Tokyo agreed to respect China's sovereignty and territorial integrity and to abandon the Tripartite Pact with Germany and Italy. When Prince Fumimaro Konoye resigned as prime minister in mid-October, a new government under General Hideki Tōjō decided to make one last effort to reach an agreement with the United States. At this point, the new foreign minister, Shigenori Tōgō, finally asked Kurusu to assist Nomura in Washington in conducting these fateful negotiations.

Despite suffering from conjunctivitis and high blood pressure, the career diplomat accepted the assignment after conferring with Tōgō and Tōjō, both of whom seemed more optimistic about possible diplomatic results than did Kurusu himself. Believing that the United States would compromise rather than face a two-ocean war, Tōjō estimated a 30 percent likelihood of success.[18] When Kurusu asked if Tōjō would support an agreement against the expected criticism from military hard-liners, the latter "declared in a firm voice that he would keep the agreement."[19] Fearing that he might be assassinated, Kurusu was accompanied by his twenty-two-year-old son, Ryo, en route to catching the Pacific Clipper being held for him in Hong Kong.[20] The world's media then chronicled his lengthy flight across the Pacific "as though he were a bird whose coming could bring fair weather or foul."[21] A British passenger on the Clipper informed Kurusu that it was "too late" for negotiations to succeed.[22] When the envoy finally reached Washington, he told President Roosevelt that "all the way across the Pacific it was like a powder keg" and thus "some way must be found to adjust the situation."[23] FDR himself would use a similar phrase—"keg of dynamite"—in his final peace message to Hirohito on the evening of December 6.[24]

Kurusu's principal task was to assist Nomura in reaching agreement with the United States through either of two propositions: In what Tōgō hoped would result in a definitive peace settlement, Proposal A pledged the Japanese government to adhere to the principle of nondiscriminatory trade throughout the Pacific, including China, so long as that principle was applied throughout the whole world. Japan would also make it clear that its adherence to the Tripartite Pact would be interpreted in terms of self-defense only and that Japan's goal was to prevent the European war from spilling into the Pacific. With regard to a Sino-Japanese peace, Tokyo proposed to retain some Japanese troops in North China, Inner Mongolia, and on Hainan Island, while pledging to evacuate all other troops within two years of a settlement. Japan would also withdraw all forces from Indochina once an equitable peace was established in East Asia. If Proposal A proved impossible, however, Togo included a second set of stop-gap terms under Proposal B. Both Tokyo and Washington would agree not to invade any area in Southeast Asia or the Pacific, with the exception of Indochina, where Japanese troops were already stationed. The two governments would cooperate in obtaining vital raw materials from the Dutch East Indies and would restore their mutual commercial relations to their status prior to the American freezing order of July 1941. The United States would also furnish Japan with "a required quantity of oil" and agree "to refrain from such measures and actions as will be prejudicial to the endeavors for the restoration of general pace between Japan and China."[25]

The most optimistic moments of Kurusu's mission came during and after his initial meeting with Hull and Roosevelt on November 17. Despite Hull's terse conclusion that "nothing new" came from the talk, Kurusu was buoyed by FDR's remark that "this Government might, so to speak, introduce Japan and China to each other and tell them to proceed with the remaining . . . adjustments."[26] That same evening, Kurusu and Nomura called on the postmaster general, Frank Walker, who emphasized that the President sincerely sought an accommodation, and if "Japan would now do something real, such as evacuating French Indo-China, showing its peaceful intentions, the way would be open . . . to furnish you with oil and it would probably lead to the reestablishment of normal trade relations."[27] Encouraged, the two envoys suggested a limited *modus vivendi* in their meeting with Hull the next day. Instead of presenting the entire Proposal B, they suggested a return to the status quo of late July, in which Japanese troops would evacuate Southern Indo-China and the United States would rescind its freezing order and resume a limited supply of oil to Japan. In reporting to Tokyo, the diplomats insisted that only such a limited agreement was possible given the time constraints. In what Kurusu deemed a "severe rebuke," however, Foreign Minister Tōgō warned that the "internal situation in our country is such that it would be difficult for us to handle if we withdrew from Southern Indo-China."[28] He instructed them to present Proposal B at once.

Perhaps the most bizarre episode in Kurusu's mission came during his private meeting alone with Secretary Hull on November 21. As the Japanese representative who had signed the Tripartite Pact in September 1940, the special envoy presented a draft document declaring that the Axis treaty "does not infringe, in any way, upon the sovereign right of Japan as an independent state" and thus Tokyo would "interpret its obligation freely and independently" and would not be obligated to "become a collaborator or cooperator in any aggression whatever by any third Power or Powers."[29] Kurusu's dispatch to Tokyo described a friendly response from Hull, who praised Kurusu's efforts to "outshine" the Tripartite Pact through a joint U.S.-Japanese effort that would bring "peace to the Pacific" and "contribute to the peace of the world."[30] In his 1952 memoir, Kurusu even recalled Hull joking to him: "It's probably customary to invite someone from afar to a dinner or golf but I'm far too busy. I realized that you can't have both golf and politics at the same time as golf takes too much time to play."[31] When they shook hands after their meeting, the secretary's hot palm led Kurusu to sense that Hull was ill. "Take care of yourself," he said.[32] Hull's version, however, differed markedly. As he noted in a brief memo of their conversation, the secretary quickly glanced at Kurusu's draft letter and "said that I did not think this would be of any particular help and so dismissed it."[33] Instead, as recounted in his memoirs, Hull thereafter "redoubled" his warnings to military and naval authorities that "Japan might attack at any time."[34] Such negativity was likely prompted by Hull's reading of a "Magic" mistranslation of Tokyo's instructions to Kurusu that erroneously obligated Japan to act "automatically" rather than "independently" of Germany under the Tripartite Pact.[35]

Hull, meanwhile, found Proposal B "clearly unacceptable," presumably because it meant that "we should have to discontinue aid to China."[36] Without formally rejecting Japanese terms, he continued conversations with Kurusu and Nomura over the next several days while at the same time floating an American *modus vivendi* to the Washington representatives of China, Britain, Australia, and the Netherlands. As Hull explained on November 22, he proposed a three-month standstill agreement whereby Japan would withdraw some 50,000 troops from southern Indochina and limit troops in the north to only 25000. In return, Washington would modify its freezing and export restrictions and resume moderate sales of oil to Japan. The secretary of state thought the odds one in three that the Japanese would accept the U.S. proposal, but if they did, it might postpone war and give the American military time to reinforce the Philippines.[37] What Hull did not realize was that the Japanese had decoded Chinese diplomatic cables and had read Hull's draft of his *modus vivendi* sent on November 22. As historian Tosh Minohara points out, Foreign Minister Shigenori Tōgō optimistically thought the Americans were preparing "a reasonable and workable counterproposal to Japan's Plan B."[38]

In what is now a familiar story, however, Hull's discussions with Allied diplomats failed to reach a consensus. Notwithstanding support from Australian, British, and Dutch envoys, the U.S. *modus vivendi* elicited only outrage from Chiang Kai-shek's government. A frustrated Hull decided to "kick the whole thing over."[39] Britain's Ambassador Lord Halifax succinctly summarized what followed: "[The] Chinks having made a proper row about the U.S. plan for a temporary agreement with Japan, Hull has apparently abandoned this . . . [and] given the Japs a general essay on high principles."[40] Instead of presenting a *modus vivendi* to the Japanese on November 26, Hull handed Nomura and Kurusu a ten-point note that restated in rather rigid terms principles for a permanent peace in the Pacific. Among the points proposed were: a multilateral nonaggression pact to be signed by Japan, the United States, China, Britain, the Netherlands, the Soviet Union, and Thailand; a similar multilateral agreement restoring the territorial integrity and equal commercial opportunities in French Indochina; the withdrawal of all Japanese forces from China and Indochina; a U.S.-Japanese agreement to support only the government of China led by Chiang Kai-shek; a renunciation of all extraterritorial rights and concessions in China; negotiation of a new U.S.-Japan trade agreement based on reciprocal most-favored-nation treatment; the unfreezing of Japan's assets in the United States; and stabilization of the dollar-yen rate.[41]

In response, Kurusu complained that the note was merely a "reiteration of the Stimson Doctrine." If he reported to Tokyo, the government "would be likely to throw up his hands." When Kurusu asked whether the Allied powers had rejected a *modus vivendi*, Hull simply replied that "he had done his best in the way of exploration." He also noted that "he might also be lynched if he permitted oil to go freely to Japan." As

Kurusu commented, Hull's note was "tantamount to meaning the end."[42] In Tokyo, the heretofore hopeful Tōgō was "shocked to the point that I was blinded by my utter disbelief" that Hull's note made no mention of a *modus vivendi* or Plan B. In a "*volte face*," Tōgō became convinced "beyond any doubt that Washington had decided on war."[43] After November 26, formal diplomacy ceased and desperate efforts to avert war commenced for the next eleven days.

As he searched frantically for possible solutions, the closest Kurusu came to assuming the nefarious role of deceitful diplomat occurred in an awkward telephone conversation just before midnight on November 27 with Kumaichi Yamamoto, chief of the American Bureau of the Japanese Foreign Ministry. The two diplomats employed a clumsy voice code that U.S. intelligence easily recorded and translated. The dialogue referred to the pending "matrimonial question" (negotiations) of "Miss Kimiko" (President Roosevelt) and whether or not a "child might be born" (a crisis or break might occur). When Yamamoto announced that "the birth of a child seems imminent," Kurusu blurted out "in which direction. . ." before catching himself. Returning again to the "matrimonial question," Yamamoto asserted, "Don't break them off." A befuddled Kurusu replied, "Not break them? You mean the talks." He continued, apparently laughing in frustration, "[T]hey want to keep carrying on the matrimonial question. . . . In the meantime we're faced with the excitement of having a child born. On top of that Tokugawa [the military] is really champing at the bit, isn't he? . . . That's why I doubt anything can be done." Yamamoto asked, "Will you please continue to do your best?" "Oh, yes," Kurusu responded, and "Nomura is doing everything too." Kurusu then added, "It is quite clear now that the southward—ah, the south, the south matter—is having considerable effect."[44] Without knowing that the Americans would read his words, a discouraged Kurusu reflexively offered his worst-case guess[45] that Japanese moves to the south into Thailand, Malaya, or the Dutch Indies would likely doom any peaceful solution.[46] Nonetheless, despite moments when he would shrug "What's the use?" the desperate envoy redoubled his quest for a last-minute miracle.[47]

On November 30, despite discouragement from Hull that "the diplomatic stage is over," Australia's minister Richard Casey called on Kurusu for a "forty-five-minute" talk that covered "familiar ground" and "may have done some good."[48] Afterward Ambassador Halifax asked Casey "to rub into the Secretary of State again [and] that I was sure that His Majesty's Government would support any interim arrangement, if such could be arranged, that was not exposed to the objections felt to earlier proposals." Hull, however, thought nothing could be done, Halifax reported, "presumably because he cannot think up any plan that would be at once tolerable both to the Chinese and the Japanese."[49] That same day, Kurusu told an American peace activist that "the last thing that the Japanese people want is war with the United States," but he warned that economic pressure on Japan might "produce an explosion"; hence, "you Americans working for continued peace must work fast."[50]

The next day, December 1, the very day that the Imperial Conference approved Japan's decision for war, Kurusu and Nomura again appealed to Tokyo to consider a possible meeting in Hawaii between Prince Konoye and Vice President Henry Wallace (or perhaps Harry Hopkins, Roosevelt's closest adviser).[51] After an interview with Undersecretary Welles on December 2, they quoted Welles's comment that Hull's ten-point note had been prompted "by the necessity to clarify the position of the United States because of the internal situation here."[52] Perhaps this was a hint that Washington might still compromise. Tōgō poured cold water on both proposals.[53]

Despite Tokyo's negative attitude, a covert opportunity presented itself in the distinguished personage of Bernard M. Baruch, the famous financier, park-bench philosopher, and friend of presidents. Kurusu did not know that Raoul Desvernine, a U.S. attorney then working on trade issues for the Japanese Embassy, had contacted Baruch through the auspices of ex-president Herbert Hoover. Desvernine had been conferring secretly with Hoover since Kurusu's arrival in Washington. When Desvernine explained that "Hull was driving absolutely toward war" but Roosevelt "was apparently holding back," Hoover suggested Baruch as the ideal go-between who might possibly expedite an agreement between the Japanese and Roosevelt without interference from the State Department.[54] With Hoover pulling strings from afar, Desvernine arranged a luncheon with Kurusu at the Mayflower Hotel on December 1, so that Baruch "could happen in and at least listen." The three men ended up talking until 5:00 p.m., "during which Kurusu went over the entire situation." Regarding Hull's note of November 26, Baruch quickly saw that it might "lead to war. And if there's a war, Japan has no chance of winning. Even if the U.S. wins, what is the victory for? No matter what, we must... avoid a war at all cost."[55] Kurusu replied that the Japanese people and "the Emperor wanted peace, but that the warlords were sitting with a loaded gun in each hand . . . determined to shoot."[56] When Baruch hesitated to act "on his own authority," Desvernine suggested that Kurusu and Nomura "prepare a memorandum along the lines discussed." Baruch could then show the memorandum to Roosevelt and say, "Here is the discussion I had with the Japanese. If you sent for them you would find out whether or not that is what they proposed."[57] Baruch later told Kurusu that Roosevelt was like "a cod-fish in water. It swims nonchalantly as if it doesn't see any bait at first. But all of a sudden, the cod-fish seizes it with its teeth."[58]

That evening, Desvernine, Kurusu, and Nomura drafted a five-point memorandum. The first point called for "a slow withdrawal of Japanese troops from China . . . under a joint Japanese and American Commission," with the Japanese retaining "three or four garrisons there, the location and size of which to be agreed upon with the United States." Point two stipulated that the Tripartite Pact would be "inoperative except in case of attack by some third power," with Japan reserving "the right to determine what [constituted an] attack." The intent was to avoid war between Tokyo and Washington "in case the United States should have war with Germany." The third point proposed that all trade and "embargoes should be settled by negotiation of new treaties of commerce covering all relationships in the commercial field." The fourth point called for an international conference "at some neutral place agreed upon" to deal with the first three issues, and that "pending the solutions of this Conference there should be an economic and military standstill agreement." Point five recommended "a relaxation of the embargo in respect to non-military commodities to be imported in normal quantities."[59]

Baruch received the memorandum initialed by Kurusu on Tuesday, December 2, and that evening, Baruch's secretary phoned Desvernine to say that "an appointment would be arranged" for the Japanese to see Roosevelt.[60] The next day, Baruch personally telephoned that FDR, returning early from the retreat in Warm Springs, Georgia, had read the memorandum and wanted "to talk to Desvernine alone." When Desvernine visited the White House on the morning of December 4, Roosevelt reportedly indicated that the memo offered "the basis for a solution." He then apparently saw the two Japanese diplomats that afternoon and again the next morning.[61] As Desvernine described it, Roosevelt even devised a way to initiate Sino-Japanese talks without becoming an official mediator. "Perhaps he might 'introduce them to Chiang Kai-Shek,'" to which Kurusu reportedly responded, "No one could refuse to meet and discuss matters after an introduction by the President of the United States." All "seemed settled," and Desvernine returned to New York on Saturday, December 6.[62] That fateful Sunday, after visiting friends in Pennsylvania, Hoover returned to New York and was greeted by two dozen reporters who asked, "Mr. President, what do you think of the war?" "What war?"

replied an astonished Hoover, six hours after Japan's notorious attack on Pearl Harbor.[63]

Most historians have overlooked the side-door interactions between Roosevelt and the Japanese via Baruch on December 4-5, 1941.[64] Diplomatic historians have focused instead on the failure to achieve an acceptable *modus vivendi* and thus conclude that Hull's restatement of basic principles on November 26 made war virtually inevitable because of Tokyo's self-imposed deadline of November 30, after which "war may suddenly break out between the Anglo-Saxon nations and Japan."[65] The Japanese envoys and U.S. officials knew of this deadline (the latter from reading "Magic" intercepts), although Hoover, Baruch, and Desvernine did not. Scholarly attention has thus centered on discussions with the Chinese, Dutch, Australian, and especially British allies as to how the United States would respond to Japan's expected attack on Malaya, the Dutch Indies, or Thailand's Kra peninsula.[66] Even Nomura's biographer, Peter Mauch, observes that after Hull's "unbending" note, the Japanese ambassador concluded that the U.S. "agreement faction" had lost out to its "firmness faction," and he then asked his government for "a declaration war" that did not arrive "until it was too late."[67] Nomura apparently did not record these last-minute communications via Baruch and Desvernine in his diary, and the one garbled reference in an intercepted "Magic" dispatch cryptically mentioned "individuals equally influential to [cabinet members] (because of its delicate bearing on the State Department, please keep this point strictly secret)" who were pressing Roosevelt "in the 'introducing' at once between Japan and China. However, the President did not make known what he had in mind."[68] Nor are there any references to these conversations in the authoritative *Foreign Relations of the United States (FRUS)* volumes and in State Department records.

Official Japanese Foreign Office documents published in 1990 suggest that Kurusu and Nomura deliberately disguised their eleventh-hour attempt to cobble together a *modus vivendi* in opaque generalities. An embassy cable to Tokyo sent on December 6 obliquely mentioned "indirect contacts with Roosevelt via his cabinet members or other influential people" and warned that "our contact with them should be kept in the strictest secrecy as they are involved without the knowledge of the State Department (and thus their identities should be kept secret)." One such intermediary, almost certainly Baruch, reportedly had lunch with FDR on December 4 and urged him to "swiftly 'introduce' the relations between Japan and China." Roosevelt, however, "did not make his position clear," an ambivalence that "was typical of the President to act like this."

The second intermediary reportedly revised the Japanese Plan B of November 20 and "included in a new proposal all the points in the previous Japanese proposal of September 25." This individual also "revised" the Hull's ten-point note of November 26 "by adding some points that were beneficial to Japan or harmless to Japan." This American thought that he could persuade Hull to "agree to the new proposal" and even contemplated "making it a new official proposal." Both intermediaries insisted that "Roosevelt still sincerely hoped that a compromise between the two countries would be made. We all know of Hull's mode of thinking and believe that it is his mental habit to over emphasize basic principles and ideals," but that Hull was always "tolerant, open-minded, and considerate about putting them into practice."[69]

As Kurusu indirectly affirmed in his postwar memoirs, this Delphic dispatch did refer in a circuitous way to the conversations with FDR facilitated by Baruch and Desvernine, but neither he nor Nomura spelled out the details of the aforementioned proposals, very likely because Tokyo had instructed them not to deviate from their instructions, warning them that "it is not appropriate for us to propose a next round of summit" or to reopen the issue of withdrawing troops from China.[70] By being vague rather than specific, the envoys desperately hoped to entice their government toward continued diplomatic discussions.

Historian Haruo Iguchi has cautioned scholars about the accuracy of Hoover's diary-narrative of these eleventh hour interactions because White House appointment logs do not list meetings with the Japanese envoys on December 4-5, 1941, nor do they confirm Desvernine's or Baruch's presence.[71] Yet it does seem clear that that the rudiments of a revived *modus vivendi* did reach Roosevelt through his old friend Baruch, as the president soon indicated to the British ambassador on the evening of December 5.[72]

A simultaneous and even more attractive option for the Japanese diplomats, especially Kurusu, was to have the President and Emperor Hirohito communicate directly with one another "as the only means of breaking the deadlock."[73] On November 28, just two days after Hull's "ultimatum," the special envoy played golf with his old friend Ambassador Joseph E. Davies. Kurusu informed Davies that unlike his impression of Secretary Hull, he had found Roosevelt "agreeable, but direct, forthright, and strong." "Mr. Ambassador," Kurusu implored, "There are only two men in the world who can possibly prevent this war—your President and my Emperor. They are the heads of state. Their actions cannot be controlled by anyone. . . . If only your President could communicate directly with my Emperor? Why cannot that be done? It must be done!"[74] Davies, who had come to like and trust his Japanese counterpart when they both served as ambassadors to Belgium in 1939, immediately "passed on" the conversation to FDR through White House aide Steve Early, emphasizing that he had "confidence in Kurusu."[75]

An even better intermediary turned out to be the well-known Methodist missionary, E. Stanley Jones, who had been importuning the State Department and the White House, as well as Japanese and Chinese diplomats, with peace proposals for the past several months.[76] In fact, Kurusu told Embassy Secretary Hidenari Terasaki that "it is your turn to become [a] betrayer," as he instructed the latter to take advantage of Jones's access both to President Roosevelt and to the Chinese Ambassador Hu Shih, and thus use Jones as a conduit to ask the president to "send a cable directly to the Emperor appealing for peace." [77] When Jones met with Roosevelt on December 3 and urged a direct communication to Hirohito, the president said that he had been considering such a message, but "I didn't want to hurt the Japanese here in Washington by going over their heads to the Emperor." When Jones confided that Kurusu and Terasaki had specifically "asked me to ask you to send that cable" because they could not do so directly without disobeying their own government, the president responded, "That wipes my slate clean. I can send that cable."[78]

It remains unclear as to how seriously Roosevelt regarded his "final message" from "the son of man . . . to the son of God."[79] In a private colloquy with British Ambassador Lord Halifax on the evening of December 5, the president reported an "indirect communication from Kurusu that matters were not yet hopeless and that direct approach to the Emperor might produce result." Kurusu had also said that "it might still not be impossible to secure a truce, and even settlement between Japan and China," and he resurrected the idea that the president could "act as 'introducer' between China and Japan." Kurusu's proposals included "a truce, withdrawal of the bulk of Japanese there from Indochina, and withdrawal of Japanese troops from North China on a time table to be agreed between the Japanese and Chinese military with an American . . . arbitrator." It was also apparent that "the Japanese would obviously want some economic relief." Without attaching "too much importance to this approach," FDR seemed "naturally reluctant to miss any chance and thought [that] communication with the Emperor would strengthen his general case if things went wrong."[80] The president nonetheless delayed several days in finalizing the message to Hirohito, weighing whether he should include an explicit war warning and also make a statement to

Congress, thereby "annoying" the British by his indecisiveness.[81] After telling Treasury Secretary Henry Morgenthau Jr. that "the Japanese were running around like a lot of wet hens," FDR gave the impression at his cabinet meeting on December 5 that the "Japanese situation seems to have eased off. Kurusu yesterday was running around Washington like a chicken with his head [cut] off and getting clergymen, Barney Baruch, and others, to rush down to the White House and recommend that various matters be reconsidered."[82]

Kurusu himself was having dinner with retired U.S. diplomat Ferdinand Mayer on the evening of December 6 when news arrived that the president had sent a "peace" message to the Emperor. The special envoy immediately commented that "this was a very clever move on the part of the [U.S.] Government; that the Emperor could hardly say 'no', nor could he say 'yes', and that this would cause many headaches in Tokyo and give much food for thought."[83] In fact, as Mayer later recalled, "Kurusu went to the very extreme limits of a patriotic Japanese in saying with the most courageous candor that anything could happen at any time, and that, therefore, the situation was one of extreme danger of war; that is to say, of attack by the Japanese government, which was then largely dominated by the militant Army group to which Kurusu and his friends were violently opposed since, as Kurusu said, war with the United States was suicide for Japan."[84] Kurusu obviously hoped to stave off war with a presidential appeal, but the fact that "things were automatically going to happen" after December 1 made it highly unlikely that Emperor Hirohito could or would do anything to halt the momentum.[85] "This is my last effort for peace," Roosevelt told the Chinese ambassador just after noon on December 7. "I am afraid it may fail."[86] Temporizing until the very end, the president toyed with including in his message to the Emperor proposals for a three-month military standstill, the withdrawal of Japanese forces from southern Indochina, direct talks between Japanese and Chinese representatives to take place in the Philippines, and "further conversations looking to a peaceful settlement of the entire Pacific area."[87] He nonetheless deleted such details when he sent his urgent peace appeal on the evening of December 6.[88] As Hull later testified, the message was more a matter of "grabbing at straws to save the peace" rather than a serious effort to resume negotiations.[89] The missive did not reach the Emperor until just before the attack began on Pearl Harbor.[90] Thus did the United States wobble into World War II.[91]

Kurusu and Nomura then became unwitting villains in a perverse melodrama played out in Secretary Hull's office at 2:20 p.m. on that

Sunday afternoon. Because Japanese embassy personnel had bungled the decoding and translation of Tokyo's fourteen-part note breaking diplomatic relations with the United States, the two envoys arrived late for their scheduled one o'clock appointment. Japanese bombs had started falling one hour earlier, and battered U.S. battleships were already settling in the mud of Pearl Harbor. After Nomura presented the note and Hull glanced at two or three pages, the latter burst out in bristling Tennessee vernacular, "In all my fifty years of public service I have never seen a document that was more crowded with infamous falsehoods and distortions . . . on a scale so huge that I never imagined until today that any Government on this planet was capable of uttering them." Hull then nodded toward the door, whereupon Kurusu and Nomura "turned without a word and walked out, their heads down."[92] The duo did not learn of the Pearl Harbor attack until they returned to their embassy.

Were the Japanese envoys surprised? Yes and no. One of Nomura's American friends, former Undersecretary of State William R. Castle Jr., later recalled the ambassador as having visited him on the Saturday before the Pearl Harbor attack and saying, "This is a farewell call. You must realize that Japan could not, with any self-respect and as an intelligent nation, accept Mr. Hull's ultimatum. I am absolutely certain, however, that, although diplomatic relations will temporarily be broken, I shall be recalled and your Government will recall [Ambassador Joseph] Grew, nothing further is going to happen. I expect to be back in Washington within a year and to have Grew back in Tokyo. Only some untoward incident could bring war, and I am certain that no such incident will happen."[93] Nonetheless, both Japanese envoys understood that if negotiations in Washington failed, "ultimately a collision with Britain and the United States owing to an attack on our part would be inevitable," or so Kurusu had informed Tokyo in his report following Hull's note of November 26.[94] As Kurusu later put it in his memoirs, "Diplomacy is akin to drawing on sand. No matter how many treaties we make or friendship agreements we sign, they will just be washed away without leaving any marks by leaping big waves, that is, . . . by just one quick action."[95] In other words, the bellicose decisions of warlords in Tokyo exposed the fragility, even futility, of diplomatic efforts in Washington.

Without rekindling conspiracy theories about who fired the first shot in 1941, we are nonetheless struck by the pervasive atmosphere of fatalism and diplomatic passivity in the final days prior to war.[96] Hull in particular showed his frustration and resignation. He complained to Ambassador Halifax that "he was pretty tired with the President's methods of being receptive to advice other than . . . the State Department's."[97] "They all come at me with knives and hatchets," he grumbled to a colleague on December 1.[98] Irascible, worn out from working sixteen-hour days, secretly suffering from tuberculosis, and convinced from reading "Magic" that Japanese diplomatic overtures were a mere pretense, Hull grew more rigid as the fateful hour approached.[99] He dissuaded Australia's Minister Casey from reviving any *modus vivendi* with Kurusu, challenged the Japanese envoys "with a great deal of bark," and argued against any direct presidential communication to Hirohito lest it be interpreted as weakness.[100] FDR also seemed "very tired," as the Japanese envoys reported, just prior to the president's "twice postponed" holiday to Warm Springs, from which he had to rush back to Washington.[101] In fact, the U.S. minster to Canada recorded after visiting with friends in Washington in early December, "Everyone [is] tired–the worst fault of the Third Term."[102] Intimates also noted Roosevelt's weariness as he resumed his White House routines, followed events at home and abroad, and delayed too long in sending the message to Hirohito.[103] With "Magic" indicating that Japan would strike southward somewhere very soon, Roosevelt and Hull seemed to view eleventh-hour proposals as clear evidence that "the Japanese are doing everything they can to stall until they are ready."[104]

From hindsight, it seems obvious that once Washington abandoned the *modus vivendi* on November 26, formal and practical diplomacy essentially ended. Ambassador Joseph Grew's postwar testimony graphically characterized the U.S. rejection and Japan's response as "the button" that set off the Pacific War.[105] In his wartime propaganda speeches, Kurusu described Hull's rejection as a lit "fuse" and a "challenge to a death fight," saying that Japan's slogan should be "Remember November 26th."[106] Hull himself apparently admitted the very next day that he had "washed my hands of it and it is now in the hands of . . . the Army and Navy."[107] As the old joke about the difference between a diplomat and a lady would suggest, when a diplomat says yes, he means maybe, when he says maybe, he means no, but if he says no, as Hull did, he ceased to be a diplomat.[108] Just four days after Pearl Harbor, Hull seemed to concede as much in an off-the-record conversation with *New York Times* columnist Arthur Krock. When the latter suggested that "we were playing for time until we could be strong enough to smash the Japs, and they found it out and smashed us first, isn't that so?" Hull agreed that "it was, putting aside the treacherous nature of the attack," and he then rationalized that "the Japanese envoys came to find out how long they could safely refrain from making war, having always intended to make it once they discovered we would not sell out China."[109] Thus, with the Pearl Harbor task force steaming toward Hawaii as early as November 25 and with the Americans rejecting any *modus vivendi* that hinted at appeasement, most scholars have agreed with Hull's retrospective judgment that the odds for any diplomatic miracle "were no bigger than a gnat."[110]

And yet we have to wonder whether Kurusu's and Nomura's eleventh-hour side-door diplomacy, either via Baruch's intervention with Roosevelt or through the Reverend E. Stanley Jones and the presidential message to the Emperor, had any practical chance of success.[111] As historian David Mayers has recently speculated, if President Roosevelt had been "more alert" he might have "mustered the imagination and means to avert war with Japan, thereby allowing a less distracted United States to confront Germany head on" in 1941.[112] As late as December 3, Ambassador Halifax noted in his diary that the one scenario that might give the Japanese "cause for pause" was if "things are really going [bad] against the Germans in Russia," but the successful counterattack by the Red Army outside Moscow did not begin until December 6—too late to change minds in Tokyo.[113] If the weary and distracted FDR had acted earlier and sent the presidential peace message to Hirohito shortly after Hull's ten point note, then—just possibly—the momentum for war might have slowed and diplomacy might have continued. Perhaps.

When Kurusu returned to Tokyo in the summer of 1942, he was rebuked by the Lord Keeper of the Privy Seal, Marquis Kōichi Kido, for "bothering His Majesty the Emperor" on exchanging messages. The special envoy downplayed his own central role by disingenuously noting that "certain individuals were working to move the president in this direction, but there seemed no reasonable way to stop this, and so we eventually saw the transmission of the president's personal telegram to the emperor."[114] Nonetheless, Premier Tōjō subsequently confided to Kurusu that if Roosevelt's message to "our Emperor had arrived just a few days earlier and the American note of November 26th had been somewhat more conciliatory, it would have been impossible for Japan to go into the war."[115] Tōjō also reportedly told General Kenryo Sato after the war that he would have accepted Roosevelt's *modus vivendi* if it had been offered: "I had already prepared a proposal with new compromises in it. I wanted somehow to carry out the Emperor's wishes and avoid war. . . . If we had only received that *modus vivendi*."[116] Of course, such Monday-morning quarterbacking understates the difficulties inherent in altering complex plans and operations at the last moment. In theory, the naval attack on Pearl Harbor could have been called off at the last moment, but as Ambassador Nomura himself pointed out metaphorically, "Big ships cannot turn around too quickly, that they have to be eased around slowly and gradually."[117] Just as militarists in Tokyo delayed the transmission of Roosevelt's cable to Hirohito, very likely the hard-liners would have blocked any *modus vivendi* once the Imperial Conference (and Emperor Hirohito) formalized the decision for war on December 1.[118] Indeed, Marquis Kido had rejected Kurusu's original proposal for exchanging messages because he believed "such a plan would result in rebellion."[119]

It is ironic that Foreign Minister Tōgō, himself a moderate who opposed the Axis alliance and wanted to avert war with the United States, took a dim view of Kurusu's belated improvisations. Tōgō believed strongly that an ambassador "conducting negotiations should exert all his personal influence and force to persuade the other party—but on the basis of instructions received." By deviating from his instructions, Kurusu allegedly "exemplified the proverb of the one who goes in search of mummies and himself turns into a mummy."[120] In short, Tōgō accused his envoy of identifying too much with his American interlocutors.[121] Yet Kurusu understood all too clearly the catastrophic consequences of war with the United States and thus bent the rules accordingly. "Both the United States and Japan were just like two children," he observed during his internment at Hot Springs. "Diplomatically they are not mature. The United States has always had a theoretical and academic approach, and Japan knows nothing of diplomacy. Japan's diplomats have never been allowed free exercise of their own judgment. If we had negotiated with England, things could have developed in an entirely different way. Now the two children are playing foolish war games."[122]

Kurusu nonetheless did express some regret over his diplomatic efforts in his second memoir published in 1952. If he had not undertaken the Washington mission, he mused, "the [Japanese] Navy would have had to bear the whole responsibility for the breaking down of negotiations and breaking out of war, with Nomura, a Navy man, so heavily involved." Perhaps the "pro-war wing of the Navy" might not have agreed to war "if the admiral [Nomura] had been the sole negotiator."[123] He even castigated himself for not openly supporting a compromise "plan immediately without Japan's approval and bear[ing] the whole responsibility for it."[124]

Perhaps the diplomat's most poignant reflection came in a personal letter to Bernard Baruch in 1947. Citing a Japanese proverb that "it is useless to keep on counting the age of your dead child," Kurusu posed an intriguing counterfactual scenario: "Suppose your Secretary of State had handed over his original plan of compromise instead of his final note, suppose again that our suggestion for an interchange of messages between the two chiefs of state should have been accepted by our government, suppose finally that your plan of solution should have been given a chance to be worked out by our government, the history of the world would certainly be turning a different course now."[125] Kurusu's desperate diplomatic efforts had failed, but the diplomat himself should be remembered as one of the few individuals, in Ambassador Grew's words, who "tried to reverse the engine, and tried hard and courageously."[126] Hailed by a fellow peace-seeker in 1941 as the "pinch hitter" who would "hit a homer in [the] last inning," Kurusu swung hard but struck out.[127]

When the special envoy returned home in 1942, he renewed his quest for peace. As Kurusu recounts in the memoir published herein, in their first meeting Premier Tōjō took him aside and asked how best to end the war following Japan's crushing naval defeat at Midway in early June. Kurusu replied—somewhat undiplomatically—that "working for peace is not as simple as starting a war." For the remainder of the war, with his resignation from the diplomatic service held in abeyance, Kurusu offered conciliatory advice as a key member of the Foreign Office Advisory Council. His proposals to terminate the war by way of negotiations with China first—and later through the mediation of the Soviet Union—were again frustrated by the military. "It was like a mouse trying to place a bell around the neck of a cat," he ruefully recalled. His last effort came in late July 1945 when Prince Fumimaro Konoye sought his counsel prior to the former premier's abortive peace mission to Moscow. With the Big Three then meeting at Potsdam, both Konoye and Kurusu anticipated that Joseph Stalin would prefer to enter the war rather than mediate. As Kurusu put it, ending the war was like "trying to borrow money from the bank with our homes in Nagata-cho as collateral without knowing that the homes had already burned down." Three weeks later the atomic bombs and Soviet intervention forced Japan's unconditional surrender. In short, Kurusu acted as a peace-seeker to the very end. A deceitful diplomat he was not.

Saburo Kurusu, daughter Jaye, and Alice Kurusu, circa 1915. Jaye married US brigadier general William Maddox after World War II, moved to Texas, and died in 1999. Courtesy of Pia Kurusu White.

Kurusu, as the Japanese consul-general in Manila in the early 1920s, pinning a medal on an unidentified US soldier. Courtesy of Pia Kurusu White.

Saburo, Pia, Jaye, and Alice Kurusu in the early 1930s. Courtesy of Pia Kurusu White.

Pia Kurusu and her father in the early 1930s. Courtesy of Pia Kurusu White.

Kurusu in the 1930s. The cherry blossoms beside him call to mind Japan's gift to the United States in 1912 of 3,000 cherry trees that still grace Washington, DC's tidal basin more than a hundred years later. Courtesy of Pia Kurusu White.

The Kurusu family meets movie star Shirley Temple in Hollywood in 1936. Eight-year-old Shirley offered ten-year-old Pia one of her pet bunnies that she kept in a kennel on the Columbia Pictures studio lot. With the family journeying to Belgium via train and ocean liner, Pia declined the gift and gave America's favorite child star a Japanese doll instead. Courtesy of Pia Kurusu White.

Ambassador Kurusu and the staff of the Japanese Embassy in Brussels, circa 1936. Alice Kurusu sits to the right of her husband, with daughter Pia at her knee. Daughter Jaye stands at the far left. Courtesy of Pia Kurusu White.

Ambassador Kurusu and son Ryo at Karuizawa in the 1930s, with Mt. Asama in the background. Ryo was killed in combat in 1945. Courtesy of Pia Kurusu White.

Ambassador Kurusu enjoying his favorite sport, archery, at his summer home in Karuizawa in the 1930s. Courtesy of Pia Kurusu White.

The Kurusu family at Karuizawa in the late 1930s. Left to right: Ryo, Alice, Pia (standing), Jaye (sitting), and Saburo. Courtesy of Pia Kurusu White.

Pia, Saburo, and Jaye Kurusu, with pet dog, Golly, in the Japanese embassy in Berlin, circa 1940. Courtesy of Pia Kurusu White.

Saburo Kurusu at approximately the time of the 1941 Washington negotiations. Courtesy of Pia Kurusu White.

Ambassador Kichisaburo Nomura (smiling on the left) and Special Envoy Kurusu (in foreground on the right), surrounded by American journalists shortly after Kurusu's arrival in Washington in mid-November 1941. Courtesy of the Franklin D. Roosevelt Library and Museum, Hyde Park, New York.

US Secretary of State Cordell Hull, who violated his own maxim by giving up on diplomacy after November 26, 1941. Courtesy of the Franklin D. Roosevelt Library and Museum, Hyde Park, New York.

Bernard M. Baruch, one of the intermediaries who helped Kurusu in his efforts to continue diplomatic negotiations in the days before the Pearl Harbor attack. Courtesy of the Franklin D. Roosevelt Library and Museum, Hyde Park, New York.

Ambassador Joseph C. Grew, who wished Kurusu well prior to his mission to Washington, DC, and later vouched for his honesty and integrity after the war. Grew sent a sincere note of condolence to Alice Kurusu in Japan when Saburo passed away. Courtesy of the Franklin D. Roosevelt Library and Museum, Hyde Park, New York.

The battleship *California* slowly sinking after being attacked on December 7, 1941. Courtesy of the Franklin D. Roosevelt Library and Museum, Hyde Park, New York.

President Roosevelt signing the declaration of war against Japan on December 8, 1941. Courtesy of the Franklin D. Roosevelt Library and Museum, Hyde Park, New York.

The Inside Story of the Japanese-American Negotiation

Our Diplomatic History

Saburo Kurusu

Kurusu's Preface

For ages, statesmen and diplomats of various nations have written memoirs, and judging even from my extremely limited experience, I realize that necessity for considerable caution in making public such a record.

In December 1939, when I assumed my post in Germany, an incident, which created a sensation within the diplomatic circle of Berlin, occurred. Ambassador Nevile Henderson of Great Britain, whose nation was then in a state of war with Germany, published a memoir of his experiences in Germany.[1] Within it were revealed the remarks made by the diplomats of such nations as Italy and Belgium, which were still on friendly relations with Germany, to the author as frank views of the group.

In view of their relationship with Germany where they were still serving, these diplomats, as a result, appeared to have been placed in a very embarrassing position. The anxiety of Ambassador Jacques Davignon of Belgium, who had been striving day and night to preserve the neutrality as a neighboring country and to prevent giving Germany any pretext for an invasion, was, in particular, very pathetic to behold.

Since Japan has finally regained her independence, it is logical to assume that anything can be written today. Nevertheless, I, as a diplomat and an individual, believe there is a standard to be observed voluntarily. I, of course, still avoid matters which, I deem, touch upon this standard, but I believe those, whose identity I did not reveal in my earlier book, will allow me to make this revelation. Also, in regards to matters of that period, which, I believe, if clarified as this time, would assist in the better understanding of our mutual position, I have clarified the detail anew.

There is a reason for my consenting at this date to the publication of this book. Since the defeat, even I, who have been living in solitude, have been hearing arguments, considerably mean and ignoring the realities of humanity. It may be that people who do not know the truth are losing their confidence because they possess no material for sound judgment.

For example, to know the truth regarding the Japanese-American negotiation may probably assist the Japanese people in reconsidering calmly once again and determining their strength and mistakes. According to my friends who have recently visited America, I am still regarded by the American people as "the deceitful Ambassador," but I would like to state that there has never been any evil design in the aims of Japanese diplomacy.[2] Even if we were to admit the mistakes committed as mistakes and the limits of our strength as limits, we after all can adjust ourselves, look toward the sun, and boldly advance into the world. Being ill of health today, I cannot write at will. Besides, due to the nature of the matters, I am conscious of numerous conditions, but I have written as frankly as permissible. I am happy that I am able to express my profound thanks in this book to those, particularly our American co-workers, who freely cooperated with us for the sake of world peace throughout the entire period of the past Japanese-American negotiation.

July 10, 1952
The author
At my home at Nagata-cho

PART I

Sketching on the Sand

"Foreign diplomacy is similar to sketching on the sand. Regardless of the treaties concluded and amity established, they are completely wiped away should the big wave of clash of national interests wash ashore. In extreme cases, doesn't the fruit of the efforts of a predecessor end in complete failure because of the doing of his successors?"[1]

Those were the words of my son, who was killed in the last war, when he decided on a career in engineering instead of continuing my works. Now, when I look back on my long diplomatic life, these words reappear in my mind.

I was about to begin writing of my various observations and experiences gained at my numerous posts. These were all priceless experiences, but they, in the final analysis, were merely writings sketched in the sand. I ended my diplomatic life with the failure of the important mission to conclude Japanese-American negotiations in late 1941. My thirty-five years in diplomacy, after all, were merely a bubble. It is useless to try to piece together the pieces of a broken earthenware, but I wonder whether it isn't a basic human trait to try anyway.

When I entered the Ministry of Foreign Affairs in February 1910, Iyemasa Tokugawa, Noboru Ito, Chokei Okaba, and Hachiro Arita, who had entered about a half a year ahead according to the results of their examinations, were already there. Thenceforth, I, as a consul at times and a diplomat at other times, moved about such places as Hankow (Hankou), Honolulu, New York, Chicago, Manila, Santiago, Rome, Athens, Hamburg,

Lima, Brussels, and Berlin. I had lived twenty-five years abroad, while my residence in Japan was about ten years, including several years as a member of the European Affairs Bureau and the American Affairs Bureau and as head of the Commerce Bureau, and the last several years of duty in the home office of the Foreign Ministry.

PART II

The Japanese-American Negotiation

Chapter 1

The Interrupted, Misread, Misinterpreted Messages

After the landing of the American troops in 1945, a considerable number of American newspaper reporters called on me at my simple mountain retreat in Karuizawa, where I had retired at the time of the termination of the war.[1] It was a period during which there are still some misgivings as to Japan's peace and order, so there were some who came around with pistols.

The reason they had called on me to such an extent was none other than to resolve their doubt as to whether I had prior knowledge of the Pearl Harbor attack. This was the question asked by practically all of the newspaper reporters.

I, of course, replied, "No," and excluding one or two of them, they appeared to have reported exactly as I had replied.[2] However, I seriously doubt the extent to which the American public, which had suspected me so profoundly since the outbreak of war, has put faith in these reports. In fact, just prior to the opening of the so-called Tokyo Trials, that is, the International Military Tribunal for the Far East, this following indeed happened.

Chief Prosecutor Keenan called me to his office in GHQ, and we stood side by side near a window, which gave a panoramic view of burned out Tokyo.[3] Stating that it probably would take fifty years to reconstruct it, he returned to his desk. Then, staring at me for a while, he blurted out: "The name the American people can hardly forget in connection with this war is not Tōgō, nor Tōjō. It is Kurusu." Then he began his interrogation.

The feeling of Americans, then, was that Kurusu had come to America for the purpose of prolonging the negotiation to gain time for Japan, and it is needless to state that the focal point of Prosecutor Keenan's interrogation was on this matter. Keenan listened to my reply very cautiously.

Then finally, pushing forward a telegram, he asked, "Do you recall this?"

As I glanced through it, such phrases as "gain a little more time" and "consult with the Navy Minister" appeared. Upon reading the entire text,

I found the message could be taken as to mean "to prolong the negotiation somewhat and consult with the Navy Minister in the meantime to do something." It was something I had no idea about. Therefore, I replied, "I don't recall having sent it."

As he insisted that it was positively sent by Kurusu from Washington on November 26, after recalling the events of that time more carefully, I reread the message with greater care. I finally came to realize that it could be my telegram suggesting a plan to break the stalemated situation through the exchange of messages between the rulers of Japan and America, but the message had been grossly twisted and grossly misinterpreted.

I replied to the prosecutor to this effect, and continuing my words, I suggested that since Japan's messages relating to the Japanese-American negotiation, together with other diplomatic messages, had all been confiscated by the Americans since the occupation, and since the original of the message received ought to be among the materials in the hands of the International Military Tribunal for the Far East, I would like to have the original translated by the translator in whom the prosecutor had the most confidence. I, too, in the meantime, would get a copy of the original, which ought to be in the Foreign Ministry, translated into English and meet with him again tomorrow morning to compare both translations. This ended our meeting for that day.

I immediately went to the Foreign Ministry and obtained and read the copy of the original message. I found the phrase "from the President to His Majesty" translated as from the President to the Foreign Minister, probably because their translator did not know the word "*sison*" (His Majesty); the phrase "obtain an extension of more time," used in the sense of requesting for an extension of the time limits, was translated as gaining more time in the American translation, and the phrase "upon referring it at least to the Lord Keeper of the Privy Seal" in our original text was translated as "to the Navy Minister."

The message shown to me by the prosecutor was probably our decoded message, which had been intercepted by the Americans, decoded into Japanese with our code obtained beforehand through some means and translated by them into English.[4] Consequently, there may have been some errors made at the time of the interception of the message, and how accurate was the Japanese code uncovered by them is not known. Besides, it probably is technically unavoidable for mistakes to occur at the time of interception and decoding. Furthermore, the degree of knowledge of Japanese of the one who did the translation is questionable. In fact, I believe only someone who is considerably versed in the Japanese language would know such a phrase as "*sison*" (His Majesty). At first I could not guess the reason for the Lord Keeper of the Privy Seal being translated as the Navy Minister. I surmised that "*Naidaijin*" (Lord Keeper of the Privy Seal)," probably had been read as "*Yonai Daijin* (Minister Yonei)" and translated as Navy Minister upon recalling that there was an Admiral Mitsumasa Yonai who had been Navy Minister some time ago.[5] At any rate, I thought that the interpretation of the message with the preconceived view that Kurusu had conspired with his government beforehand to betray America had led to such an odd mistranslation and the translation of extension of time as gaining time.

The next day, taking along the translation of the original message translated by an expert from the translation section of the Foreign Ministry, I again met Prosecutor Keenan. Before I could say anything, he frankly admitted the mistranslation of the message and added that he had taken steps to have the records of the United States Senate corrected.

When the truth of the mistranslated message became clear, the prosecutor's attitude toward me softened markedly. Prosecutor Keenan also said this: "In America, the demand for calling Emperor before the court is great. Wouldn't there be anything that would prove the Emperor was not responsible?"

Therefore, I again promised to verify the fact. Since this message was being considered to have a great bearing on the Emperor's responsibility question, I made every effort within my power to clarify this point.

Therefore, I had Secretary Hidenari Terasaki, who was then doing the interpreting for the Emperor, inquire as to whether he had seen our messages, and it became clear that the Emperor absolutely had no knowledge of them. I therefore immediately relayed this fact to the prosecutor.[6]

This was before the opening of the Tokyo Trials and several months before the prosecutor had expressed the opinion that "Even if the Emperor had had attempted to stave off the war. . . ." I have no idea as to what extent the prosecutor's cognizance of the Emperor's responsibility question, which had gradually deepened in such a manner during those few months, affected the Tokyo Trials.

Later, as the Tokyo Trials progressed, it was gradually revealed that this was not the only message of ours which had been misread and misunderstood by the Americans. The one deemed the most important was the misreading of Tokyo Dispatch No. 726, dated 5 November. I will explain this somewhat when I deal with the progress of the negotiation later, but our authorities have gone so far as to say that this mistranslation caused America to break off the negotiation and was, in the final analysis, the important and direct cause leading to the outbreak of the war.[7]

It is being said that it is hardly possible, after all, for an envoy, who had been hurriedly flown with such an important responsibility at such a critical time just prior to the outbreak of war, not to have an accurate knowledge of what would follow in the event of his mission's failure. This deduction is indeed reasonable as a conclusion reached within a country having a normal political structure and under normal conditions, but no matter how I may try to deny it, it is exceedingly difficult for me to convince others.

At first, I tried to explain in various ways, but I finally gave it up as hopeless and decided to leave it to the judgment of the International Military Tribunal for the Far East. I described this mental attitude in a paragraph of a letter, dated 7 July, 1948, and addressed to Bernard M. Baruch, a prominent figure in the political and financial circles of America, as follows:

"I presume that there are many Americans who are still persistent in their belief that I had been dealing with the American side with a treacherous intention of giving a false sense of security, in order that the Pearl Harbor attack might be successfully carried out. Quite naturally, I have been very anxious to deny such mistaken charges. As a matter of fact, at several press interviews after the war, I tried to refute such accusation most emphatically. But I was very disappointed to find out that the public prejudice is still too strong and any denial on my part can do very little to rectify wrong impression.

However, now the International Military Tribunal for the Far East is functioning in Tokyo. Many eminent judges and lawyers from various allied nations have been working for more than one year for the investigation of war crimes. They have all important evidences on their hands, and every witness they desire is ready to respond to their call. All telegrams exchanged between us and Tokyo are in their possession, completely deciphered and translated, and I have already been questioned several times by the judges of the prosecution section. But so far I have not been indicted on any charge of war crime. I presume if my name may yet be left out of the list of the accused at the end of the trial, even those who have been most persistent in their suspicion will then be convinced that I was not guilty.

Confidently waiting for such a day, I am now quietly living in retirement in this mountain resort. It is a rather trying affair and calls for a great deal of patience and sacrifice on my part and that of my family. But after all it is the price I naturally have to pay for the risk I volunteered to take, in my eleventh hour effort, to save the situation for my country. Under such circumstances, I beg to assure you that it has always been a source of great encouragement to think that a man of your wide and varied experience in state affairs believed in my integrity all through our collaboration."[8]

Bernard M. Baruch formerly held the important position of chairmanship of the Atomic Energy Commission, but his most active period was during World War I.[9] He gained prominence as President Woodrow Wilson's right-hand and as head of the War Industry Board, he established the war footing of American Industry, and directing it freely, he showed its strength to the world. He was over seventy years old in 1941 and well known throughout the world, and his relationship with President Roosevelt was very close. Until the Japanese-American negotiation was broken off by the Pearl Harbor attack, he listened to our earnest request and exerted every effort toward the conclusion of the negotiation. I will discuss his friendly efforts later.

Chapter 2

The Midnight Messenger

It was midnight of 3 November 1941. I was fast asleep from the fatigue of having walked at the exhibition at Ueno with my son during the day, when I was rudely awakened by the visit of a policeman from the Kojimachi Station. As our phone was out of order, he had come as an urgent messenger of the Foreign Minister to relay the message that I was wanted immediately at the residence of the Foreign Minister.

On hurrying to the Foreign Minister's residence which was not so far away, I found Foreign Minister Shigenori Tōgō, Vice-Minister Haruhiko Nishi, Kumaichi Yamamoto of the American bureau, and Toshikazu Kase of the 1st Section, American Bureau, all with a tense look standing in the large drawing room on the second floor, which was fully lighted in spite of the fact that it was midnight. It appeared as though they had just concluded an important conference.

On that occasion, the Foreign Minister first explained, in general terms, the state of the Japanese-American negotiation and then requested me to go to America at this time as a special envoy and to do my utmost in helping Ambassador Kichisaburo Nomura to conclude the negotiation.

As Foreign Minister Tōgō had resided, as I did, in Karuizawa prior to assuming his present post, there were many times when we had discussed the question of Japanese-American negotiation. As to his view then, he once stated that I should go to America in such an event and handle the negotiation. However, in my first talk with Tōgō after he had become foreign minister, he stated that the previous Foreign Minister had already made numerous commitments to the military and others in regard to the Japanese-American problem and that in view of the decision of the Imperial conference of 6 September, in particular, his scope of action as foreign minister was so restricted that the sending of a special envoy, as he had thought of doing during the time in Karuizawa, was absolutely impossible. Consequently, I was greatly surprised that night when he asked me to go to America as special envoy.[1]

Now, according to his explanation as foreign minister, America's attitude in the negotiation has continued to be unyielding with no signs of any conciliatory attitude.[2] Furthermore, since America's economic pressure is becoming increasingly great, our country has been placed in a predicament wherein she must devise some drastic measure to break the deadlock. Since the deployment of our military strength, provided for an emergency, would become known sooner or later and if that should happen, the Japanese-American negotiation would inevitably become much more difficult, it must be said that the situation, from an objective state, was already in a dangerous state. As to whether there was time to devise some sort of plan for changing the situation at this time, it seemed that the scope of possibility of a compromise was gradually shrinking in substance and in time and with the practical cessation of traffic on the Pacific, he thought at first that the idea of sending a special envoy must be abandoned completely. "However, if we, with the cooperation of American, can have the Clipper schedule postponed two days and can have you board it, we believe that there is still time to make a final effort before the deployment of our military strength becomes apparent and causes the negotiation to become much more difficult."

Then, as a logistic order, he began to explain the concrete plans of settlement, that is, Plan (A) and (B). Plan (A) dealt with (1) the question of non-discrimination of trade, (2) interpretation of the Japanese-German-Italian Tripartite Agreement, and (3) the question of American attitude in the negotiation had continued to be unyielding with respect to troop evacuation, all of which were the crux of the negotiation.

The main points were that (1) should he applicable not only to China, but to the rest of the world, (2) be interpreted as Japan having no obligation to support Germany and Italy in arms should America, based on her rights of self-defense, go to war against Germany and Italy, but America should not needlessly enlarge her interpretation of the rights of self-defense, and (3) be explained that troops will be stationed in North China, Mongolia and on Hainan Island for a necessary period of time, while the evacuation of troops in other areas will be completed within two years after the establishment of Sino-Japanese peace, and French Indo-China will be evacuated immediately following the settlement of the Sino-Japanese incident or the establishment of a just peace in the Far East.

Plan (B) contained the following four essential points.

(1) Japan and America will agree to make no armed advancement into Southeastern Asia, excluding French Indo-China, and into the South Pacific area.

(2) Japan and America will cooperate with each other to guarantee the acquisition of raw materials from the Netherlands East Indies.
(3) America will restore the Japanese-American trade to the state existing prior to the funds freezing act.
(4) America will agree to supply Japan with the necessary quantity of oil.

So long as a special envoy is going to be sent anew, the usual practice would be to take along some sort of a new plan for breaking the deadlock, and I believe it would be most effective, as a diplomatic tactic, to propose the plan at a "psychological moment," such as the special envoy's first meeting with the President.

With such an expectation, I listened to the explanation of the concrete plans. However, according to the Foreign Minister, since time was so urgently pressing with not a moment to be lost, time would not permit the envoy to carry the new plans nor present them upon his arrival in Washington. Consequently, both plans would be immediately cabled to Ambassador Nomura.

Then, on studying Plan (A) and (B), I thought that since both plans were comparatively simple in their formulae, we might be able to discover some sort of basis for an understanding within a short time in spite of the pressing situation today.[3] In regard to Plan (B), in particular, I had heard from Yoshida that an almost identical plan had been drafted by such elders as Shigeru Yoshida and Kijuro Shidehara and although most unofficially, the opinions of the American and the British Ambassadors had been sounded, and that the response of the British ambassador towards it had been interpreted as rather promising.[4] Therefore, I was inwardly happy that Foreign Minister Tōgō, who I had heard was not interested in it, had finally come to suggest it and considering it together with the assistance of the British ambassador, of which I had also heard, I thought that we might be able to find a clue for the development of the situation somewhere in this neighborhood.[5]

It is needless to state that since the mission was of such great importance, I thought that they should have selected the most qualified from among the numerous experienced elder statesmen. But the situation, as explained by the Foreign Minister, was so pressing that there would be no time at this late date to look for and make overtures to the right man. And as the means of traveling would be to fly across the Pacific, I thought it would be practically impossible to ask of an aged elder statesman. I decided there was no one but myself to do it, so I replied, "I'll accept it."

This is something that happened later, but when I heard from Secretary of State Hull, upon my arrival in America, of the cooperation he had received from our delegation, Viscount Kikujiro Ishii[6] and Eigo Fukai,[7] at the London Economic Conference of 1933, I regretted very much the hasty action of our government and the fact that we were not able to trouble such an elder statesman as Ishii, who had the confidence of the people, both at home and abroad.

It was under such circumstance that I came to accept such an important mission, but it can be said that I already had the background before the decision had reached this stage.

According to the plan I had from the time I was head of the Commerce Bureau, my idea was that it would be very desirable to obtain the mediation of Great Britain, where China policy is considered to be very practical because of her wealth of experience in regard to China and her substantial practical interests such as investments and trade, to effect a break-through in the Japanese-American relations, which had deteriorated considerably particularly since the Manchurian Incident. Already during my tenure as Ambassador to Belgium, I often had assisted Ambassador to Great Britain Yoshida and later Ambassador Shigemitsu in trying to improve our British relations centering around the China problem.[8] I even had the experience of having had some response during Chamberlain's premiership, but missed in capitalizing on it. When considered from these facts, this mission can be interpreted as having presented me with my last opportunity to achieve my ambition. The reason I had placed considerable hope in the attitude of the British Ambassador toward my plan, which resembled Plan (B), was due to their circumstances and considerations.

Furthermore, immediately after the creation of the 3rd Konoye Cabinet, I was asked by Foreign Minister Teijiro Toyoda to assume the post of vice-minister and assist in the Japanese-American negotiation.[9] At that time, I had a rather favorable impression of the attitude of Foreign Minister Toyoda, but due firstly to my principles regarding participation of military men in foreign diplomacy and secondly to the warning from Dr. Kakinuma regarding my blood pressure and heart, I frankly explained my reasons and refused. Soon afterwards, I was asked for a written opinion on the settlement of the Japanese-American problem, which I submitted. Let me give you a brief outlines of the substance of that opinion.

With the Japanese-American relations having deteriorated cumulatively over a number of years, the President of the United States cannot be expected to change his present attitude toward Japan, which he has steadfastly maintained, unless something extraordinary happens. Consequently, with the deterioration of relations causing Japan to evacuate her citizens, excluding the Nisei, residing in North and South America regardless of how many years it may take, Japan should, at this time, eliminate the two great causes of the Japanese-American conflict by suggesting to buy up or swap the assets and interests of her citizens in North and South America with America's interest in China, which was at issue, and then conclude a non-aggression treaty or a treaty for the disposition of conflicts. If America failed to agree to this proposal, our just position then could become clear to the world. At any rate, it cannot be denied that such circumstances as these of the past caused me to decide to accept the mission.

Having finally decided to go, I felt that I was not familiar with the recent developments of the Japanese-American negotiation and needed to catch up on it, as I had been living in seclusion in Karuizawa since my return from Germany. Therefore, I requested the selection of a secretary who would be familiar with the details of the negotiation. As a result of a conference with the Vice-Minister of Foreign Affairs and members of the Administrative Bureau, who were present, it was decided that it would be best to trouble Shiroji Yuuki, former head of the 1st Section, American Bureau, who had recently been transferred and was on a leave-of-absence status. That evening's discussion was concluded with the agreement that Kase, head of the 1st Section, would seek the assistance of Ambassador Joseph Grew of America in regard to the important matters of having the Trans-Pacific plane delayed and securing a reservation aboard it.

To secure passage for Japanese aboard Trans-Pacific planes, at that time, reportedly was practically impossible. Hence, to have a schedule changed was thought to be a very difficult matter, but preliminary arrangements were completed. It was about 2 a.m. when I received the necessary documents and returned home. I still remember the surprised look of my family when I asked them to hurriedly prepare my traveling gears for a trip to America upon returning home.

The following morning was spent in studying the documents and listening to the explanations of the officials concerned. I obtained a rough idea in regard to the details leading to the sudden aggravation of the negotiation, which had been proceeding comparatively smoothly in the beginning, through the occupation of the southern portion of French Indo-China by our troops in late July and the pending difficult points, namely, the claims of both parties concerning the problems of non-discrimination of trade, interpretation of the Tripartite Agreement, and evacuation of troops, listed in Plan (A).

In the meantime, I learned that Foreign Minister Tōgō had reported the matter of sending me to America to the Emperor through the Premier and also received the report that the American Ambassador had consented to use his good office in securing passage aboard the plane and had wired the request to the Department of State. It became known in the afternoon that American officials had agreed to delay the schedule of the Clipper and to hold it with a seat for me in Hong Kong. Then, my trip to America finally became certain.

Then, I made various arrangements with Foreign Minister Tōgō. As it was revealed then that Plan (B), explained the night before, would actually be presented by me upon my arrival in Washington, I felt that it had become somewhat easier for me to work in that respect. I, also, had a talk with Taro Terasaki, head of the American Affairs Bureau, who was then constantly in touch with the General Affairs Bureau of the Army and the Navy and heard from him his very encouraging suggestion that I should not hesitate to call upon him for anything should a possibility for a Japanese-American compromise be recognized, and in such an event, he would attempt to sway the army and the navy even in the evacuation of troops problem, which he regarded as the most difficult of all.

Chapter 3

My Meeting with Premier Tōjō

Thus, that evening at 7 o'clock, I called Premier Tōjō at the war minister's residence. Until that evening, Premier Tōjō was a total stranger to me. The only occasion I had had was when I was asked to assume the presidency of the Bureau of Information at the time of the formation of Tōjō's cabinet and I refused. This negotiation, too, was a conversation by phone from Karuizawa with Naoki Hoshino, who became the chief secretary of cabinet. Hence, this was my first direct meeting with Premier Tōjō.

The Premier, it seemed, had just made himself comfortable following his busy day at the office, as he was in his kimono and "hakama."[1] Firstly, he told me that when he had reported the matter of my going to America that day, the Emperor had said, "But I have heard that he was in ill health." This probably had entered his ears at the time I refused the post of vice-minister of Foreign Affairs. I could not help but be greatly moved by such thoughtfulness by the Emperor, who had cared to remember such a trifling personal matter.

This is something else, but at the time I refused to accept the post of vice-minister of Foreign Affairs, I had been firmly dissuaded by Dr. Kakinuma because of my high blood pressure and a severe case of conjunctivitis. Another reason for my refusal was my principle. I believe that military men should not take part in politics. Consequently, I thought that it was a mistake for one, who was the oldest member of the Foreign Ministry, to serve as vice-minister under a military minister. I, of course, am speaking of Toyoda.[2] It was not a problem affecting only myself. I thought that such combination would be the cause of mistakes. And in view of Foreign Minister Toyoda's desire, I stressed only my reason based on health.

During the course of discussion with Premier Tōjō that night, it was revealed the Prime Minister had the same opinion as the Foreign Minister and myself in recognizing this proposed mission to be an extremely difficult one. But given that, (1) America's preparation for war on both oceans was still insufficient, (2) America's public opinion was not supporting war, and (3) America's provisions for such important war materials as tin and rubber were insufficient, he believed Americans willfully would not look for war. He repeatedly emphasized that I should strive for a compromise as he believed the possibility for conclusion of the negotiation to be 30 percent for success and 70 percent for failure.[3] Furthermore, I still remember him saying that of the three knotty problems of the negotiation, the question of evacuation of troops was one in which no concession should be made and that if any concession should be made in this matter, he would not be able to face toward Yasukuni Shrine and sleep.[4]

Therefore, I frankly stated that I believed his opinion regarding the possibility for conclusion of the negotiation to be too optimistic and that I had dared to accept this difficult task only because I believed that I would have no excuse to make to the Emperor and the nation were I not to exert my utmost effort to break this deadlock. Then, I queried him as to what would happen if the negotiation should proceed the way it had done to date and war should break out. The Premier replied that he was certain that we would not lose during the opening phase of the war and did not attempt to say anything more.[5] To avoid tying up my hands from the bullish attitude he might assume were I to press him further, I changed the subject.

I stated that I believed this mission to be extremely difficult and asked if he would doggedly support and carry out the compromise reached by us even in defiance of the strong opposition of various circles within our country, which inevitably would crop up, in the event a compromise should be fortunately be reached. To this, the Premier promised in a reassuring tone that he would certainly carry it out.[6]

As we were about to end our discussion, the Premier added that for various reasons, the negotiation must be concluded by the end of November and instructed that he wanted this message relayed, at least, to Ambassador Nomura. As a so-called "time limit" was now attached to my work, it became much more difficult. There was nothing to be done about the deadline now as I had already accepted the position and the Emperor had been informed of it. I renewed my determination to go to America and exert my utmost to the very end.

Just before taking my leave, and apologizing that it might sound impolite to the Premier, who was an army man, I frankly reminded him that I thought the so-called "national solidarity" advocated by the military to date was scare tactics—forced national solidarity based on fear of the military—and was absolutely not our genuine feelings, and I stated that the premier's recent attempt to convene an emergency session of the Diet and to inform the nation of the realities of the situation was a very appropriate action. To this, there was no response.

When I called on Ambassador Grew at the American Embassy and thanked him for his assistance in connection with the plane problem, he inquired as to who my accompanying secretary would be. When I replied that it was to be Secretary Yuuki, he expressed his satisfaction of the cooperative spirit displayed by Yuuki as section head and promised to continue his effort to obtain passage for the secretary.

Furthermore, Ambassador Grew inquired if I was taking along a new plan of settlement. When I replied negatively, he, with a very disappointed look, stated very frankly that it would be useless for me to go. Now I explained that if we had such an ingenious scheme of settlement, as anticipated by the Ambassador, today when the situation was so extremely critical, I believed it would have been wired to Washington immediately without waiting for my trip to America; that our government was sending me to America with the idea that "no stone should be left untouched" at this time for the sake of preserving peace; that in view of the fact that the negotiation for both America and Japan had been discussing the same points over and over for the past six months in Washington, it can be thought that the negotiation might have fallen into a set pattern, and there was no telling that some new phase might not be developed through my participation, Ambassador Grew appeared to have been convinced for the first time.[7]

As Mrs. Grew appeared as I was about to leave the Embassy, I shook hands with her and said her good-bye.[8] She was shedding tears. I was deeply moved with an indescribable emotion as I imagined the feelings of Ambassador and Mrs. Grew, for many years, who had exerted their every conceivable effort toward Japanese-American amity, while seeing me off at a time when the relationship of both countries was facing a crisis.

Later that evening, I, using an automobile, called on Hachiro Arita and Shigeo Yoshida, in the order named, to exchange views and entrust with them the affairs of my home during my absence. Arita had experienced in contacting and negotiating with the military while serving as head of the Asia Bureau, vice-minister of Foreign Affairs, and foreign minister several times. And as he was familiar with the latest movement within the military circle, he, being concerned for the worst, explained his various views and gave me advice. As I expressed my conviction that since I had already accepted the mission and the Emperor had been informed of it, I should do my utmost for the sake of peace at this time. Arita came to appreciate my point of view.

Since Yoshida and I had always been working together with the same idea ever since we had been in Europe together, and been associating frequently as he, too, lived in Nagata-cho, we understood each other well. Our exchange was simply "Well, I am going," "Return as soon as possible."[9]

I returned home at midnight and after a short nap, I headed for Tokyo station at 4 a.m.[10] Accompanied by my secretary, Yuuki, and well-wisher Shimazu, private secretary to the Foreign Minister, and Ryo, my only son, I headed for Otsubama aboard the first train for Yokohama.[11] After a short rest at the Air Corps Headquarters, we were placed aboard a medium sized navy bomber and headed straight for Formosa.

It certainly was a hurried departure, as only 20 and some odd hours had elapsed from the time I was asked to accept the mission to the time I departed.

Chapter 4

Passing through the Places of My Two Years of Service

Accompanied by Secretary Yuuki, from Otsubama I boarded a medium sized navy bomber early on the morning of 5 November. Our first schedule was to land at Taihoku (Taipei), but due to the weather, it was hurriedly changed and we landed at Chuyuan Air Field near Takao (Kaohsiung) on Formosa (Taiwan). As Chuyuan was a naval air station, there were numerous planes standing wing to wing. The behavior of the officers and men in station was indeed spirited, fully revealing their daily training and an aspect of the critical situation.

After entering the air station headquarters and paying courtesy to Commander Tsukahara, who reportedly had lost an arm in an air attack over Hankow, we were to be billeted overnight in an inn arranged by headquarters. We took a hot bath to relieve our fatigue from the early morning and enjoyed the atmosphere of a Japanese inn, our last for some time to come. The next morning, we were again aboard a bomber and flew to the Sixth Naval Base near Amoy. From there, we went to Amoy (Xiamen) aboard a small steamboat.

Guided by the consul, we toured the city of Amoy until the departure of the ship for Hong Kong sometime after midnight that night. I spent the time in sympathizing with the diligent efforts of the Portuguese to remain neutral while interposed between Japan and China and in visiting the gambling house called the Monte Carlo of the Orient.[1]

We finally boarded the ship at midnight, and it was on the morning of the seventh that we arrived in Hong Kong. As my trip to America had been reported in the newspapers the day before, it seemed that a big crowd had gathered at the wharf. I boarded an automobile together with Consul-General Yano, who had come to greet me, and winding through the crowd, we headed for the point of departure of the plane for Manila. While in the automobile, I was told that the navy's determination to keep troops on Hainan Island was unyielding. I boarded the small plane flying between

Hong Kong and Manila for the trans-Pacific plane passengers and landed at Cavite at about 2 a.m.

Generally speaking, America, considering the Philippines as her base for advancing into the Orient, has been sending navy superior men, but it was the tendency of Japan, despite its proximity, to be neglectful. This was the place where I had served for two years as the first consul-general about twenty years ago when Japan's policy was changed and the consular status was raised. Consequently, I had many friends, and since Conrad Penites, who, together with Consul-General Katsumi Niiro and the representative of local Japanese residents, had come to greet me on the order of President Manuel Quezon, a friend whom I was meeting for the first time in twenty years, our hand-shake became vigorous of its own accord.

Because of my long years of residence abroad, Manila was a place of reminiscence. Consequently, even during the short interval on my way to Manila Hotel, where I, led by Penites, who came to greet us, registered as guest of President Quezon, various memories of twenty years ago returned and made me feel wistful.

Soon after having established myself at the hotel, I called on President Quezon. Led by an adjutant (Laurell's son), who spoke fluent Japanese and reportedly had studied at the Military Academy in Japan, I entered the President's chamber. Quezon welcomed me with an attitude short of embracing me.

My talk with Quezon, needless to say, primarily dealt with my mission to America. As we talked of our family's welfare, then some of our friends and Quezon's experience of two years of sickness, we practically did not know where to stop. In the meantime, Vice President Sergio Osmena came and our talk again returned to my mission. Quezon expressed great concern for the future of Japanese-American relations from the standpoint of a Filipino. I explained to him that the Japanese government was sincerely striving for the success of the Japanese-American negotiation and requested for the lateral support of influential Filipinos, including Quezon.

This talk did not touch on any problem in detail, but was merely an exchange of general views. During the conversation, Quezon revealed that the Philippines had been definitely promised independence in 1946, regardless of the outcome of the Japanese-American negotiation.

Then, I called on High Commissioner Francis B. Sayre at this official residence. This was not my first meeting with Sayre. On my way to assume my post in 1936 when I was appointed Ambassador to Belgium from my post as head of the Commerce Bureau, I had discussed with Sayre, who was then the second Under Secretary of State, two or three matters dealing with the Japanese-American cotton agreement and the taxes of three Japanese steamship companies, which were my unsettled affairs as head of the Commerce Bureau.

From the time of this negotiation in Washington, I had the idea that High Commissioner Sayre, together with Secretary of State Hull, was a champion of the principle of free trade and that there existed a very close relationship between the two. I had heard, also, that Sayre had visited Japan during the time of Admiral Yonai's cabinet and had exchanged views with Foreign Minister Arita for the solution of the problem pending between Japan and America. As he was well known as President Woodrow Wilson's son-in-law, I, thinking that to obtain Sayre's understanding eventually might contribute to the progress of the negotiation in Washington, very frankly listed the reasons why I thought my mission was very difficult. I explained that he could readily see how pressing the relations between Japan and America was by merely looking at Manila today with its elaborate military preparations.

Sayre, then, wondered if I wasn't being too pessimistic. Hence, I explained my view. Since the Washington Conference, some of the Chinese, considering the Nine Power Treaty and other agreements as white paper mandates for anti-Japanese movements and hastily concluding our country's conciliatory diplomacy as evidence of the weakening of Japan under the pressure of England and America, have been depending on American and immediately carrying out anti-Japanese policies. As a result, the Japanese-American relations, not to mention the Sino-Japanese relations, have always been drawn into a vortex of war. Thus, the cause of the Japanese-American difference was complex and also deeply rooted. Nevertheless, America, without considering this fact, has been stubbornly trying to carry out her usual Chinese policies, it seemed, through her economic pressure against Japan. Such being the case, the settlement of the Japanese-American problems cannot help but be regarded as very difficult, and this was the reason I was concerned about the future of the Japanese-American diplomacy.[2]

Secretary Lawrence Salisbury, who was present, expressed a similar opinion concerning the misconception of some Chinese in regard to the Washington Treaty. He was an old friend of mine dating from his undergraduate days at the University of Chicago.[3] Not only had he been studying Japan for many years and was very fluent in Japanese, but he also was well acquainted with the details of the Sino-Japanese problems as he had served both in China and Japan. Since he was well known as a man who expressed very harsh criticism toward our diplomats concerning the actions of our military toward China, I felt very reassuring when he expressed a similar opinion as mine in regard to the Washington Treaty.

I, then, continued that America appeared to think that she could bring Japan under submission eventually through the abandonment of the trade agreement, the freezing of funds, and the charge on the export of important products to Japan, but this was a very dangerous point of view that ignored our national characteristics. I explained that the Japanese from old had a tendency always to choose honorable defeat rather than ignominious safety when confronted with danger and having to decide the next move. In regard to honorable defeat, I repeated its full meaning in Japanese and requested Secretary Salisbury, who was fluent in Japanese, to translate it.

After Sayre, in replying to this opinion, had explained the principle of world peace based on his pet theory of free trade, I retaliated and stated that leaving aside the question of the high tariff policy of America, herself, for the time being, I believed that the economic bloc policy, carried out by England since the so-called Ottawa Conference, was wholly contrary to the contentions of High Commissioner Sayre. Sayre explained that England's policy and position after the war probably would change considerably and that she probably could not continue such a policy.

In other words, this discussion, too, had no concrete substance, but enabled me to realize fully that America, as usual, possessed a steadfast commitment in regard to the problem of the Open Door in China, which was one of the difficult points in the Japanese-American negotiation.

Later, I held an interview with foreign and Japanese reporters in my room in Manila Hotel just prior to attending the reception sponsored by Consul-General Niiro. The questions fired at me by the reporters were manifold, but the principal point appeared to have been whether I was taking along a new plan of solution at this time. Of course, I had replied "no" to this.[4]

The reception sponsored by Consul-General Niiro was attended by many Americans and Filipinos. High Commissioner Sayre had Admiral Thomas C. Hart, Commander-in-chief of America's Far Eastern Fleet, were there. When my old friend, Gen. Emilio Aguinaldo appeared, I remember seeing the old general, who was leaving early, off at the entrance. Since this get-together was purely a social affair, I can't recall with whom I had talked on that occasion. However, High Commissioner Sayre appeared to have repeated his principle of free trade even on that occasion. While talking to Admiral Hart at this reception, I jokingly remarked, "In other words, I am going to negotiate to make you become unemployed." As this was accidently overheard by a reporter, it appeared to have been reported as news.

Just as the reception was about to end, Quezon sent his private secretary to tell me that he wanted to talk to me once more. Quezon was an admirer of Gen. Douglas A. MacArthur as a man of character from old and often had expressed this during my tenure of office in Manila. Since he, during our discussion that day, had urged me to meet the General once, his business of that evening might have been this. However, since I couldn't find the time for it, I lost my chance to talk with Quezon again forever.

When the Japanese-American war finally broke out, Quezon, it seemed, visited America, making speeches at various places, including the Congress, and holding interviews with newspaper reporters. During my internment, I read these newspaper accounts with special interest and I felt very reassuring to find out that he, as usual, was exhibiting his keen political intelligent everywhere.

This goes back to many years ago. It happened when I had completed my tenure as Counsel-General at Manila and was leaving the Philippines. A reporter, who was aboard the Santo Albano, on which I was, sent out a dispatch stating that I was one who held the independence of Philippines to be premature. Quezon, who read of this in the newspaper, became very indignant, it seemed, for later when he met me again in Japan on his way, if I remember correctly, to America, he immediately mentioned this article and rebuked me. I purposely replied that I, as stated in the article, thought that the independence of the Philippines was premature. Quezon, with a dubious look, asked me why. I asked him in return whom he would want as Japan's first ambassador if the Philippines obtained her independence. As he replied, "You, of course, "I replied, "Look, I am merely a consul-general and it will take me some time to become an ambassador. That is why I believe the independence of the Philippines premature." We both had a big laugh out of it.

As he was concerned about even such trifling newspaper reports, the contribution made by Quezon toward the achievement of the Philippines's independence was indeed outstanding. I often had heard from numerous Filipinos and Americans, including Governor General Burton Harrison, of the effort exerted by him from the time he was the Philippines' representative in Washington to the time of the passage of the Johnson Law and even after that.[5] I always had a great respect for his fighting spirit, and the fact that he talked about his two years of fight against illness in our conversation that day was, in other words, a manifestation of his passion to fight for the independence of the Philippines even unto death. Today when his aim of many years has been completely achieved, I cannot help but be deeply moved on thinking that he, who had devoted his entire life to this movement, was now resting in Heaven.

After our defeat, I heard that Manila, which holds many fond memories for my family and myself, had been completely destroyed and that Intramuros, Luneta, and Escolta were practically ruined. To this destruction will become attached a very understandable enmity and an inevitable hatred in view of the loss of many of their loved ones, such as parents, husbands, wives, brothers and sisters, and the trampling of their dignity. On considering what the sentiment of the people of the Philippines will be toward the Japanese in the future, I, who had preached Japanese-Philippine friendship to Quezon for many years and had advanced it up to my last visit to Manila, cannot help but be appalled at the development of such a pathetic reality.

Chapter 5

My Forty-Eight Hours at Midway

The following day, November 8, our plane left the Philippines. After stopping overnight at both Guam and Wake, it arrived at Midway on the tenth. As one of the four motors have developed trouble on the way, we were forced to remain on the island for about forty-eight hours.[1]

In regard to our overnight stops at Guam and Wake, we arrived at each island in the evening and left early the next morning. Since the routine was to be greeted by an officer of the American Garrison Force, exchange greetings and go to bed almost immediately after diner, I had no opportunity to talk with the other passengers. But since at Midway we unexpectedly had time to spare due to the engine trouble, the commanding officer of the American Garrison Force purposely came for me at my hotel on the evening of the day after our arrival. He entertained us with a dinner at the barracks and movies in the open after dinner. As luck would have it, a squall came in the midst of the movies and we took shelter in the commanding officer's room. The commanding officer, trying to entertain us with news from Tokyo, tinkered repeatedly with the radio, but did not succeed. I, however, would not help but express my whole-hearted thanks toward the kindness of the commanding officer, who strove so hard to help me beguile the tedium of my journey on this isolated island in the broad Pacific expense of water.

As I had time on Midway, I talked with a Sir William J. "Tony" Keswick of Jardine Matheson Company of Shanghai, who was one of the passengers.[2] In regard to my mission to America, Keswick stated that it was too late. According to the other passengers, he had the status of private secretary to Duff Cooper, and since he was on his way to London after having recently completed an inspection tour of the Southwest Pacific area with Duff, I listened with special attention to his comment that it was too late.

I also talked with another passenger named James, a Canadian, who had resided in the Kwansei area for many years and was well known among the Japanese and whom I had met once or twice before. James stated that he would like to assist me in my mission as much as possible. According to what he told Secretary Yuuki, there were many British and American military men among the passengers, and their opinion was that the British and Americans residing in the Far East no longer desired an adjustment of relations with Japan through conciliation. They were angrily stating that real adjustment of relations was impossible until the Japanese army was crushed. Because of the humiliation they repeatedly had suffered from the Japanese army before the Chinese since the Sino-Japanese incident, they, led by a band, had paraded through the streets of Shanghai. This, in all probability, must have been the honest feeling of numerous Americans and English men who resided in the Orient at the time.[3]

To me, the most important event that occurred during my stay on Midway was Prime Minister Churchill's speech, made in London directly on the other side of the world. According to the radio news, which I had on the island, he reportedly stated in his talk at a luncheon for the mayor of London at the Mansion House on 10 November that should America become involved in a war against Japan, England would declare war against Japan within an hour.

Through this statement, England's conception of the Japanese-American negotiation became clear. As I had explained previously, I had heard before I left Tokyo that the British Ambassador had manifested an interest and understanding toward a Japanese-American conciliation plan similar to Plan (B), but that was merely the personal opinion of the Ambassador. It became clearly evident through this speech of the British Prime Minister that my idea of expecting British assistance in the Japanese-American negotiation must be given up entirely.[4]

According to what I heard from Toshikazu Kase, the head of Section 1, American Bureau, after I had returned to Japan aboard the exchange ship in 1942, he was asked by the British Ambassador Sir Robert Craigie when he had talked with him immediately after the outbreak of war, if Kurusu's trip to America was really for the purpose of peace. When he replied in the affirmative, the Ambassador, after stating that he himself had believed it to be so, reportedly spoke reminiscently that his conscience also was very clear as he, too, had exerted his utmost effort for peace to the very end. In all probability, Ambassador Craigie, too, must have continued suggesting plans for the preservation of peace to his government up to the very last moment.[5]

As I had explained previously, it was my idea from the time I was head of the Commerce Bureau that the development of Japanese-American relations should begin from the improvement of Japanese-British relations. Even when Lord Francis Barnby's party visited Japan and Manchuria in 1934, it was my desire to help the party achieve its mission and this, too, was based on this contention.[6]

The head of the Military Affairs Bureau there was General Tetsuzan Nagata.[7] It was unusual for the head of the Commerce Bureau to call on the War Ministry, but I called on Gen. Nagata. I strongly emphasized that we, following the example of the late Count Shimpei Goto, should take the initiative to invite British and American capital and techniques into the development of Manchuria. And should American and British capital obtain a place of security and British and American trade find a profitable market through the development of Manchuria, America's and British's appreciation of our China policy would improve. And from the standpoint of promoting investments and trade, Japan's position as the stabilizing power in East Asia, too, would gradually come to be understood by various countries. I, also, urged the army's cooperation in support of Lord Barnby's party.

Gen. Nagata immediately showed signs of agreement, but stated that he would reply after having discussed it first with the members of the Bureau. As expected, Lt. Col. Tasumi was sent to the Commerce Bureau that afternoon to inform us of the decision to purchase the iron needed by the Manchurian Railway from England for the time being as a means to assist Lord Barnby's party in the objective of its visit. Thus, the Military Affairs Bureau cooperated with us in striving its realization, but the authorities of the Manchurian Railway's accountant's Department stubbornly opposed the plan, claiming that British rails and other products were costlier than our domestic products. On investigating, it was found that Yawata was supplying those products below market price since the Manchurian Railway was their best customer, but they would rather sell to others. In spite of this fact and since they would not submit their estimate even on the orders of President Yosuke Matsuoka, we had to devise other various plans. I drafted a special subsidy plan to augment the temporary loss to be suffered by the Manchurian Railway from the purchase of the British products, and this was presented to Chief Secretary Rocock of Lord Barnby's party by me just as they were about to sail for home from Yokohama. Since Rocock, however, refused to consider it on the ground that purchases through special plans ran counter to the usual course of trade and had no permanency, our hope finally was not realized, but I was impressed by that decision.

Later, when I was appointed as Ambassador to Belgium, Shigeru Yoshida received his new assignment as Ambassador to England, just about the same time. As we had been exchanging views often, I knew that he was planning to promote the readjustment of our relations with England with practically the same idea as I had. Because of this, he even urged me to come to England as his advisor, citing the example of Enjiro Yamaza of the Political Affairs Bureau, who cheerfully went to London as an advisor in 1908. In the end, I promised that though I would be serving in Belgium, I would visit London often and help Ambassador Yoshida with his work. Ambassador Yoshida and I left for our new posts in Europe by way of America a ship apart.[8]

It was in about May 1936 when we assumed our posts in Europe. With a People's Front government being established in France and a revolution breaking out in Spain, the political situation in Europe at that time was very confusing. In November of that year, Japan signed the Japan-German Anti-Comintern Pact and in July of the following year, the Sino-Japanese incident broke out, soon spreading to Shanghai and causing the British Ambassador incident.[9] Not long afterward, the Sino-Japanese incident became the problem of the League of Nations. Then, the Nine Power Conference was convened, followed by the successive outbreak of the *Panay* sinking and the *Lady Bird* bombardment incidents. As a result, the atmosphere enabling us to improve the Anglo-Japanese relations never did present itself.

However, there appears to be many reasons leading us to believe that the sincerity and efforts of Ambassador Yoshida were fully appreciated by the British. It was at this time that Ichiro Hatoyama, Ambassador Yoshida's friend, exerted his lateral effort for the readjustment of the Anglo-Japanese relations by visiting England as a party politician and exchanging views with Foreign Secretary Anthony Eden.[10]

As 1938 came, Ambassador Yoshida finally left London and was succeeded by Ambassador Shigemitsu. On the request of both Ambassadors, I was to continue rendering my assistance in the British plan and was asked to attend the transferring of duties between the two Ambassadors in Paris. In the meantime, Prime Minister Chamberlain's appeasement policy was gradually being carried out in England, and after the famous Munich Conference, we received a report that there were indications that England would assume a conciliatory policy toward Japan, too. Therefore, it was decided that I, who was in the independent position, would feel her out, and arrangements were made for Mr. A. H. F. Edwards, an

Englishman, who, having spent many years in China, was familiar with the Far Eastern situation and who had been assisting in the contacts between our Embassy and the British authorities previously, exchange frank views with me concerning this problem.

In mid-November of that year, we met at our Embassy and held a three hours discussion. According to the records at hand, the outline of this discussion was as follows:

1. It probably would not help improve the immediate situation even if the discussion on the Anglo-Japanese relations were to go far back into the past. The procedure would be to plan for the solution of the pending problem, namely the question of protection of our mutual interest in China, after the creation of a friendly atmosphere through the readjustment of relations between the two countries in compliance with the present situation, that is, the reality that Japan is moving and fighting with a big army, instead of from the formal argument as to whether a declaration of war exists.
2. England seems to be advocating for the restoration of the Sino-Japanese relations to be the status quo ante based on the Washington Conference, but it was because of the existence of a great defeat in this status quo ante that the Manchuria and the Sino-Japanese incidents broke out.
3. With the situation such as it is today with Japan and Great Britain always struggling and opposing each other because of the China problem, Great Britain will be compelled to aid China, regardless of whether she wants to or not, because of her interests in China. Hence, some of the Chinese, constantly hoping for this intervention, are boycotting Japan and drawing Great Britain into the Sino-Japanese conflict. Since the Anglo-Japanese relations, not to mention the Sino-Japanese relations, and the peace of the entire East Asia are being continuously threatened, the utilization of British interests in China in such a manner by a third powers should be prevented through the adjustment of the Anglo-Japanese relations.
4. To recognize Japan's special position in regard to China is, in other words, merely to approve the existing situation and if, as an unreal problem, funds for investigation in China were to be solicited from among the British investors, in general, those investors will seek a guarantee that their investment will not become involved in another maelstrom, such as the current incident, through a Sino-Japanese or an Anglo-Japanese conflict and will inquire as to the understanding

of Japan. From this point of view, it is believed the best policy to cope with the present situation would be to recognize Japan's peculiar position and to establish a policy to prevent Sino-Japanese conciliation.

As a result of this discussion, a private plan for an Anglo-Japanese pact embracing the following three points, was drafted.

1. Recognition of Japan's peculiar position in China.
2. Establishment of a joint Anglo-Japanese committee on the spot for the solution of the problem concerning the protection of interests.
3. Settlement of all further conflict through peaceful means.

Mr. Edwards took this draft and left. Later, claiming that he had obtained a general approval of the leaders of the British government in regard to this plan, he expressed a desire to continue the discussion with me. As I was unable to comply with his request because of matters I had to attend in the country I was serving, I had Ambassador Shigemitsu continue it and returned to my post in Brussels.

Later, Ambassador Shigemitsu, appearing to doubt the advantage of relaying this plan in its entirety to our government, seemed to have modified it considerably and made it into a vague thing lacking a concrete plan in his dispatch to the government. To this dispatch, our government replied that the time was not ripe for our British plan.[11]

According to the explanation made by the then Foreign Minister Hachiro Arita after the war, there were a great number of advocates of a German-Japanese military alliance within our military circle ,and since it was all that the government could do to barely check them along the line of the Anti-Comintern Pact, to bring forth anew the Anglo-Japanese problem and cause the situation to become more confusing was an absolutely impossible proposal.

Thus, our plan for the adjustment of our relations with England finally fell through. Later, in December of that year, the American government sent a note to the effect that she would not recognize any indiscriminate interference into new situation and the changing of a treaty without formal procedure. About a month later, the British government followed with a note of a generally similar nature. Nevertheless, Foreign Minister Halifax stated before the Parliament that Great Britain was prepared to enter into a negotiation for the adjustment of the Anglo-Japanese relations centering around the China problem, but Japan did not give it any consideration.

Later, as a result of the Tientsin Incident and the Burma Route problem, the Arita-Craigie agreement was concluded, but since it was merely a local understanding, it was far different from the fundamental adjustment of the Anglo-Japanese relations which we were striving for.[12] However, since that agreement, too, was immediately counteracted by America's notification of the abrogation of the Japanese-American Commercial Treaty, my idea of placing our hope in the support of the British must have been mistaken from the very beginning. Therefore, just as claimed by Keswick, the time probably was already too late. At any late, the statement of the British Prime Minister, which I had heard of while on this isolated island, was indeed a great disillusionment to me.

In the meantime, my stay on Midway reached its second day. During the day, I listened to the practice of the anti-aircraft guns being fired in front of the hotel. Then, I was told by the commanding officer of the American Garrison Force that arrangement had been made for a navy plane to come from Hawaii for me, should the repairing of the Clipper plane take longer. Fortunately, however, the repairs were made and leaving early on the morning of the twelfth, we arrived in Pearl Harbor that afternoon. As we were about to land, blinds were placed completely over the windows, shutting off the view of the harbor and indicating a truly rigid manner of a security.

Upon landing at Pearl Harbor, I was immediately surrounded by numerous reporters. Some of them promptly questioned me in regard to Prime Minister Churchill's speech. Although I tried to dodge it as though it were nothing, I certainly had the feeling that they had hit upon a vital point. From Pearl Harbor, I went to Honolulu together with the welcoming officer aboard an automobile sent by the American authorities, and we lodged at the Royal Hawaiian Hotel on Waikiki beach. Thirty years ago when I had served for eight months in Hawaii as a junior vice-consul, I had lived in a house on the beach near this hotel. The sound of the waves caressing the beach and of the wind among the leaves of the coconut palms brought back many memories. As I, invited by Consul-General Nagao Kita, dined only with my old Japanese resident friends, I practically had no contact with Americans in Honolulu.[13] I merely had conversations with Secretary Colville, who was on his way to succeed Secretary Salisbury when I had met him in Manila, and with a reporter, who was heading to Tokyo as correspondent of the *New York Herald Tribune*.

The following day, the thirteenth, I boarded the California Clipper, a considerably larger plane than the one I had been on, and headed for mainland America. I arrived in San Francisco after having slept overnight in the sleeping compartment of the plane. As was expected of in mainland America, the number of reporters and others who were there was considerably larger, and I had great trouble in replying to their questions. At any rate, I struggled through safely and accompanied by Consul-General Yoshio Muto, who had come to greet me, I went to his official residence to rest. The Consul-General appeared to have worked hard in the selection of the planes I was to ride from here. Finally, it was decided that I would go to New York aboard the so-called "strato Liner," which flew very high.

This plane appeared better equipped than the California Clipper, and I fell soundly asleep in the soft nice feeling bed. Not knowing when I had flown over Chicago, I arrived at LaGuardia Airfield in New York the following day, the fifteenth. I was greeted by Consul-General Morito Morishima and others, but the number of reporters was surprisingly few, indicating that they were waiting for my arrival in Washington. After resting and gossiping with the Consul-General and others at the air field, I got aboard another plane and arrived in Washington.

As I looked about while getting off the plane, there appeared to be a great crowd on the airfield. Among the crowd, I soon saw Ambassador Nomura as well as members of the Embassy and the local Japanese residents, who had come to welcome me. I also saw that even my old friend Joseph Ballantine from the Department of State had come to greet me. There were a large number of men connected with the newspapers, the movies, and the radio, waiting for me. No sooner had I gotten off the plane, I was asked to give my impression before a microphone. After pictures, broadcasts, and interviews, I finally passed through the gate and arrived safely at the Embassy.[14]

At the Embassy, I entered the room on the second floor that was assigned to me as my room, and after having put away my baggage and cleaned myself; I briefed Ambassador Nomura and Minister Kaname Wakasugi with the details of my trip, the atmosphere in Japan, and the gist of my instruction. I also met the members of the Embassy and the Japanese reporters, who were waiting.

When I finally returned to my room, I felt really exhausted, both mentally and physically. As no plane reservation could be obtained at first for Secretary Yuuki, who had accompanied me, he had left Tokyo with the intention of accompanying me to as far as Hong Kong. Hence, he had arrived in Washington with only his clothes on his back and my briefcase.

Chapter 6

Washington at the Time of My Arrival

The day following my arrival in Washington was Sunday. As Ambassador Nomura, accompanied by Minister Wakasugi, had conferred with Secretary of State Hull the day before, it was decided to confer with the President and the Secretary of State on the 17th with the addition of myself. Therefore, I was able to spend the entire day of the 16th in a leisurely talk with Ambassador Nomura.

As Ambassador Nomura had served many years ago as a naval attaché assigned to the Embassy in Washington, we had known each other since then, but because I was in Chicago then and our duties and posts differed, this was the first time that we were to work closely together. Nevertheless, it was Ambassador Nomura, who as Foreign Minister in the Abe Cabinet had appointed me Ambassador to Germany. Besides, on my way back from Germany the previous spring, I had had the experiences of listening to the progress of the Japanese-American negotiation, although it was then only at the beginning. Furthermore, as I had heard that he, during the regime of the 3rd Konoye Cabinet, had requested of Foreign Minster Toyoda my assistance in Washington with the statement "A person like Kurusu, for example."[1] It was not certainly a strange coincidence that I was to assist Ambassador Nomura.

Nonetheless, compared to the time when I had stopped over in Washington on my way back from Germany, the situation had changed markedly. It became clearer once I heard directly on the spot that the entire matter had become aggravated—particularly after the occupation of Southern French Indo-China by our troops in late July.

Therefore, the question was how to change and develop the situation. Plan (A), which was shown to me by the Foreign Minister just prior to my departure from Tokyo, had already been presented by Ambassador Nomura. Only in regard to the question of non-discrimination of trade was a comprehensive counter-proposal made and sent to us as of the 15th. It became evident that it was absolutely hopeless to expect the prompt acceptance of Plan (A) in its entirety by the other party, as had been expected by our government. Furthermore, the Foreign Minister's telegraphic instruction[2] dated 5 November and apparently wired just after my departure from Tokyo, read: "For various reasons, it is necessary to have the negotiation signed by the 28th of this month at the latest. Although this is like asking for the more difficult, it absolutely cannot be helped due to the surrounding situation." Not only was the time limit of "by the end of the month," which was issued by Premier Tōjō just before my departure from Tokyo as an instruction meant for just Ambassador Nomura and myself, the time was now further shortened, and the agreement had to be signed, too. Hence, we on the spot were placed in a position where we had to request of our government a little more time and, simultaneously, to break the deadlock confronting us in some manner even if we had to deviate somewhat from the final plan issued by our government.

What most fully describes the position of those on the spot and the mental state of Ambassador Nomura then is the dispatch[3] sent to the Foreign Minister by the Ambassador just before my arrival, that is, on 14 November. The gist of this cable, which appears in Ambassador Nomura's book, was as follows:

1. America's Pacific policy lies in further obstructing our northward and southward advances through her economic oppression. On the other hand, she is gradually proceeding with her military preparations.
2. America would rather fight than yield her foundational political principle, which is her creed, and regards Germany's prosperity to be on the downward grade.
3. Her relations with China are closer. Hence, the China problem will become the stumbling block to stability in the Pacific.
4. The view considering the Axis relationship as a means to stab America in the back is gaining strength daily.
5. Our southward advance eventually will result in a war with the Netherlands, America, and Great Britain with the strong possibility of Soviet Russia's participation.
6. The war will be a protracted war.
7. Since America's Pacific war will be primarily "convoys," the concentration of her main strength in the Pacific is possible. American isolationist sentiment against war with Japan is weaker than against war with Germany.

With this premise, it continued: "Although I am not fully aware of the present situation in our country, I am aware of the urgency of the situation through your successive dispatches and although I may be criticized as being rather unreasonable to make such a negotiation as this in as much as I am aware of the fact that the nation, too, is beginning to lose its patience. I believe that it would be wiser to remain patient, if the situation permits, until the outlook of the entire world situation becomes a bit clearer rather than to wrangle for a delay of a month or two."

The situation at the time of my arrival was, in general, like this, but we had not given up hope. In fact, Ambassador Nomura and I even had discussed the matter of who was to return to Japan in the event the negotiation was concluded. I claimed that it was only proper for the one who had come as special envoy to return, and Ambassador Nomura insisted that he should return to make the report. After all, we both know how badly Delegate Jutarō Komura had been received upon his return from Portsmouth after the Russo-Japanese war.[4] As it was likely that the objection of the nation would be greater in this instance, I fully sympathized with the secret resolution of Ambassador Nomura.

Amidst such an atmosphere, together with Ambassador Nomura, I called on Secretary of State Hull on the 17th and accompanied by the Secretary of State, we went to the White House. With the Secretary of State present, we thus began our first negotiation with the President.[5]

Besides holding frequent formal negotiations, once more since that first one with the President (November 27), 10 times with the Secretary of State (November 17, 18, 20, 21, 22, 26, 27 and December 1, 5, and 7) and once with the Under-Secretary of State Sumner Welles, we had two private discussions with Postmaster General Frank Walker and several meetings with Bishop James E. Walsh, who had been assisting us from the side in this negotiation, and the Rev. James M. Drought (who had been my fellow passenger aboard the plane from Manila). And as I will explain later, we obtained the understanding of several other influential individuals to work from the side.

In regard to the details of the negotiation, they are dealt with in Ambassador Nomura's book and the messages exchanged between our government and us, I believe, will be made public sooner or later, but since there are things I saw and felt regarding the negotiation after my participation in it, I would like to describe them based on the dispatches of that time.

The dispatches relating to the discussions with the President and the Secretary of State following my participation were dictated to and recorded by Secretary Yuuki immediately after the discussion before my memory had a chance to fade. As I read them today, they bring back many memories and recollections.

Chapter 7

My First Meeting with the President

At 10:30 a.m. November 17, accompanied by Ambassador Nomura, I entered the office of the Secretary of State at the Department of State and held my first discussion[1] with Secretary of State Hull. This was not the first time I had met Secretary of State Hull.

On my way to assume my post as Ambassador to Belgium in 1936, I paid my respects to Secretary of State Hull when I discussed with Assistant Secretary of State Sayre several matters, which were my unfinished business as head of the Commerce Bureau. On that occasion, I heard his opinion concerning free trade.

At the opening of our discussion, Secretary of State Hull, exhibiting a very austere attitude, explained that the present world situation had been brought about by a lack of far-sighted statesman in the world following the First World War, and we must now find a way to save the world from the recurrence of such misfortunes.

Therefore, I replied that from that point of view, I believed the responsibility of both Japan and America, who fortunately were not involved in the European war, to be great and explained the details leading up to the instructions from the Prime Minister and the Foreign Minister ordering me to America. I further explained that the Prime Minister's desire for peace was so strong that it probably would surprise the Americans and that on the three problems which were the difficult points of the negotiation, he was fully inclined to compromise, except on the third question of stationing of troops.[2] As the time for the meeting with the President had approached just then, we, together with the Secretary of State, headed for the White House.

This was the first time I had met the President. My impression of the President was what a cheerful and broadminded individual he was and that he amidst his unaffected airs possessed the appearance as to be expected of one who came from a blue-blooded American family. If I were to look for a similar type among our country's statesmen whom I know, it would be Prince Fumimaro Konoye adorned with American-like vitality and vigor or perhaps more accurately if I were to say a combination of Prince Konoye and Lord Shigenobu Okuma.[3]

I explained to the President, as I had told Secretary of State Hull, about our government's desire for peace, and sought his understanding of the present frame of mind of our people, who had seen four years of the Sino-Japanese incident. I further stated that judging from the military situation I had seen on my way to America, even I, a layman in military matters, could see that the situation was very pressing and in such a state as would explode into crisis should one false step be made. I asked what would Japan and America gain by bringing about such a situation. The President, expressing a similar opinion, promptly replied, "Yes, what for?"

I continued and explained that what we should note at this time was the question of "time element," and should the negotiation be prolonged any longer, Japan's position would become graver, both economically and militarily, eventually leading to her total submission. Consequently, the Japanese people were worrying about this, in particular, in the anxious frame of mind explained previously.

In reply to this, the President, quoted the famous remark "There are no last words between friends," made by Secretary of State William Jennings Bryan to Ambassador Sutemi Chinda when Japanese-American relations had become strained because of the California land question many years ago. He thus made it clear that America had the intention to continue the negotiation to the very end and stated that in the event it became possible to conclude an agreement between Japan and America, he preferred a general understanding since he believed nonaggression pacts to be outmoded.

Taking up where the President left off, I replied as follows: In concluding such an agreement, the question of reconciling it with the Tripartite Pact and also with the past claims of Japan concerning the China question would arise and should America insist that the Tripartite Pact be abrogated, Japan would not be able to agree to it as a matter of national dignity, but it cannot be thought that America, who constantly claims to respect international treaties, would take such a stand. Since the Tripartite Pact, to begin with, is aimed at the localization of the war situation and the preservation of peace, we believed that from this very fact, it would be possible to find such points of reconciliation.

In regard to the China problem, I replied that no matter how good it might sound to America, it would be impossible for Japan to promise something she knows she cannot do in view of the situation on the spot. I explained my claim, which I had revealed to High Commissioner Sayre in Manila on my way to America and which can be termed my pet theory, that is, the reasons why the Washington Treaty and Japan's subsequent conciliatory diplomacy were being interpreted as Japan's submission to Great Britain and America and have caused the stirring up of anti-Japanese movements in a section of China. I suggested that even in regard to the Sino-Japanese peace question, so long as America interferes even in setting terms and manifests such attitude as to support China, it would be very difficult to reach a conciliation between Japan and China.

The President replied that he had heard of the difficulty of evacuating the troops because of the Sino-Japanese question, and as he stated, "I don't know whether such a word as this is used diplomatically, but how would it be if America were to be the "introducer" for both Japan and China? There would be no need for the introducer to meddle into the substance of a talk, but to bring both parties together," I answered that it was a splendid idea.

Then, I touched upon the Tripartite Alliance. I explained that I had heard that some Americans had misinterpreted Japan's explanation to America that the execution of the obligation of the Tripartite Pact would be determined according to her own interpretation as meaning to stab America in the back whenever Japan found it convenient, but that was a gross misinterpretation. I stated that this explanation already indicated that Japan would never become the tool of Germany, as thought by some Americans, and that the Tripartite agreement would be outshone if a general Pacific agreement, as suggested by the President, should be concluded. Consequently, I believe that the question of the application of the Tripartite Pact would vanish of its own.[4]

At this point, Secretary of State Hull interjected and explained Germany's ambition toward South America. He stated that it was a certainty that Germany would attack America with the conquered British navy after having conquered South America and setting up puppet regimes everywhere, that America must set up her defense plan now since it would be too late to do anything when that happens, and that Japan should be able to understand this. Supporting the Secretary of State, the President explained that the Central and South American map, of which he had spoken in his recent talk, was the real thing obtained from German government sources.[5] Therefore, I retorted that considering even from the fact that one side of the western hemisphere faced the Pacific Ocean, it did not mean that Japan would be partner to the disruptor of peace in the western hemisphere. I further explained that since Japan had already declared that should a general Pacific Ocean Pact be concluded, she would withdraw her troops from French Indo China following the establishment of peace in the Pacific. Therefore I believe that the disputed evacuation of troops from French Indo-China would then materialize and enable Japan to actually prove to the American people her peace policy, which is also desired by America. I also stated that some Japanese, however, would recall the fact that Japan, which had fought as a member of the Allied nations during the previous World War, had been tormented in various ways at the Pacific conference and others after the war and thus demanded a guarantee on this point in connection with the conclusion of a general Pacific Ocean pact, as suggested by the President. The President promptly replied, "Let us cover it all."

Hence, Secretary of State Hull suggested that this matter be further discussed. He stated that he and Ambassador Nomura had discussed this matter many times and since it seemed that they, too often, were only revolving around the same point, he would like to hear Kurusu speak from a new angle. He indicated that it would be alright if they returned to the Department of State and continued the talk. However, it was finally decided to continue the talk at the Department of State the following day. Ever since that moment, I have regretted that I did not accept Secretary of State Hull's proposal and continued the discussion with him immediately after the talk with the President.

Since I was the new participant in this discussion with the President, it had been desired that I would be the principal speaker for Japan, and as this, after all, was an important first meeting, I worked very hard. Considering such matters as the time limit, in particular, I strove very hard to induce a speedy conclusion of the negotiation by impressing strongly upon America the urgency of the situation and, at the same time, was very careful in the usage of my words to avoid giving either party a feeling of "intimidation." However, my hope for the future of the negotiation was strengthened because of the statesman-like attitude of the President, the proposal for a general agreement, and the use of such a word as "introducer."[6]

Chapter 8

My First Negotiation with Hull

The following day, the eighteenth, together with Ambassador Nomura, I conferred,[1] as scheduled, with Secretary of State Hull. At first, the crux of our discussion was the Tripartite Agreement, but since an important proposal was made by Ambassador Nomura during the midst of the discussion, this first meeting became a very important one from the standpoint of the development of the negotiation.

The Secretary of State first explained the reason why he became concerned about Hitler's movement earlier than the American public. He explained that this aggressive movement did not know where to stop, that America, too, would eventually become its objective, and that he found it very difficult to understand why Japan could not realize Hitler would advance into East Asia after his complete victory.

He then vigorously attacked the atrocities of the Nazi in various countries and the insincerity of the Germany's diplomacy, and he pointed out that she already has been insincere toward Japan twice, first in the German-Soviet Pact and then in the German-Soviet war. He explained that America's policy of peace and Nazi Germany's policy of aggrandizement through military strength fundamentally contradicted each other, that Japan's alliance with Germany must be considered to be the greatest barrier to the adjustment of Japanese-America relations, and that should America conclude an agreement with Japan, some Americans would inevitably denounce it as America's submission to Germany's saber-rattling policy indirectly through Japan under this circumstance.

Continuing his argument, the Secretary of State declared that even if an agreement were to be concluded, under the present circumstances, it would mean nothing as it would only lead to an accumulation of military expenditures for both countries in as much as both would continue to increase their military strength and oppose each other, as in the present Japanese-Soviet relations.

In other words, of the three difficult problems of the negotiations, what America placed the greatest importance on was the question of the Tripartite Alliance. In order to conclude a general agreement as suggested by the President yesterday, America wanted the problem of the Tripartite Alliance liquidated first as this would completely eliminate her apprehension of the possibility of being stabbed in the back by Japan, regardless of how the European situation changed in the future. I was able to fully understand how profound Secretary of State Hull's feeling of antipathy toward the Nazis was through his expressions and tone when he criticized the Nazis.

I realized that as I had stated at yesterday's conference, it was impossible to promise something that could not be done, no matter how good it may sound to America and that even if America demanded an invalidation of the Tripartite Agreement, that would be an impossible proposal. The Secretary of State thereupon replied that America was not in a position where she could demand the invalidation of the Tripartite Agreement, and that although it was understandable to himself as to why Japan wanted to cling to the Tripartite Pact on one hand and seek a Japanese-American agreement on the other hand, it would be difficult to make the American public understand it. I then explained the reasons why the aim of the Tripartite alliance was not aggrandizement through arms, but he merely retorted that assurances meant nothing unless the purpose was actually proven.

Thus, the situation became one of both parties bandying words around the question of the Tripartite Alliance, which had become a cancerous growth in the Japanese-American negotiation as well as for Japan herself.[2] It was at this point that an important proposal was made by Ambassador Nomura.

The gist of Ambassador Nomura's proposal was as follows: We believed that it would be very difficult to solve immediately the fundamental question of what should be done with the Tripartite Alliance. Should Japan's and America's disposition of military strength be increased during the period of this discussion, would it not eventually lead to an unfortunate incident? Hence, the urgency of the moment would be to leave aside for the time being the arguments over lofty idealistic views and attempt to alleviate the tense atmosphere. For this purpose, how would it be for both to restore the situation to what it was prior to the freezing of funds? That is, for Japan to withdraw her troops from Southern French Indo-China and for America to rescind her foreign funds freezing act. Should the atmosphere of both nations be alleviated, it would become unnecessary to send warships to Singapore and to strengthen the defense of the Philippines. We then could resume our negotiation.

This proposal was one that further contracted Plan (B), which our government had instructed would be our final plan. It was indeed a bold proposal for us at the spot. I had held the same opinion for some time and I thought it only proper from the atmosphere on the spot and on Ambassador Nomura's position and his troubled state of mind. With the time limit requiring the signing of an understanding by November 25th drawing near at hand, we were confronted with an absolutely hopeless situation of softening America's attitude quickly. So long as he desired peace, there was no other alternative than this for the Ambassador, who practically was standing on the cross-road of peace or war, hoping to break the deadlock.

Secretary of State Hull was very cold even to this labored proposal of Ambassador Nomura.[3] He refused to approve it, stating that it would be useless to undertake such a temporary measure before the fundamental question has been settled, and that although America would like to see Japan take the leadership among the nations of East Asia, she believed the saber-rattling policy controlling Japan to be an impediment to world peace. As Ambassador Nomura and I prevailed upon him in return, he finally stated that he would not mind persuading Great Britain and the Netherlands to consider restoring the situation to that which existed prior to the enforcement of the funds freezing act, if the leaders of the Japanese government would clarify the extent to which they would carry out the peace policy.

We then touched upon the question of evacuation of troops and non-discrimination of trade, but he did not press too much on the question of evacuation of troops. The Secretary of State's idea in regard to the trade question was that since there inevitably will be an opposition between the non-discrimination policy and totalitarianism in connection with the economic restoration following the war, he would like to have the cooperation of Japan at that future time.

What became clearly evident through the President's meeting of the day before and the Secretary of State's meeting of the following day was that America was considerably enthusiastic about concluding an agreement with Japan and acting as "introducer" between Japan and China, but to bring this about, it would be necessary to dispose of the Tripartite Alliance question in some manner and to conclude a Japanese-American treaty that would be understandable to the American people in regard to the question of non-discrimination of trade. But what could we do in view of the government-ordered time limit? To develop a situation wherein the signing could be done within that time limit was absolutely impossible. We thought that the only alternative left would be to seek for the approval of our government concerning the plan proposed by Ambassador Nomura at this discussion. Therefore, immediately after this discussion, I sent a cable[4] containing the following point as my personal observation:

1. According to our observation, the President appears to be fully enthusiastic regarding a Japanese-American conciliation. Consequently, don't hastily conclude America's failure to accept our plan as a dilatory tactic and undertake any irreparable action.
2. With the recent amendment of the neutrality act, America's concern has turned toward the Atlantic and although she is determined to fight against Japan, if inevitable, she would rather obtain security behind her back through a pact with Japan, if possible. We believe the reason the President and the Secretary of State have come to place greater emphasis on the Tripartite Alliance and make claims stronger than in the past on this point in recent discussions is because of the situation mentioned above.
   As a promise for a Japanese-American conciliation, we believe that she is seeking a declaration of a Japanese-American pact in regard to the principle of non-discrimination of trade or a message of a responsible individual expressing Japan's peaceful intentions in order to give the American people an impression of cleavage in German-Japanese relations.
3. Although it may be impossible to radically change the German-Japanese relations, it would be advisable for our country, even when the post-war situation is considered, to make America feel at ease in some manner at this time and allow her to pay greater attention to the Atlantic area.
4. Even if we cannot undertake immediately measures following along this lines desired by America at this time because of our domestic situation, we believe that in view of the time limit, to have America rescind her funds freezing, as suggested in Ambassador Nomura's proposal of the 18th, and obtain a guarantee of a specified amount of oil supply is of urgent necessity for the breaking of the deadlock. As compensation, we hope that such readiness as to begin withdrawing troops from French-Indochina attached with such vague terms as no

> expansion will be made beyond French Indo-China or withdrawal of troops will be made after the establishment of a just peace, as stipulated today. If possible, I would like to have this swiftly disposed of before the President leaves Washington on the 20th.

While waiting for the reply from our government to this request, we repeatedly heard reports that America intended to give favorable consideration to Ambassador Nomura's proposal of the 18th. The following morning, the 19th, Bishop Walsh, who had been assisting Japan in various ways from the beginning of the negotiation, called on me at the Embassy. After relaying the information that America would probably accept Ambassador Nomura's proposal, he congratulated us on the accomplishment of our mission and shook my hands firmly. Then, on the evening of the 19th, together with Ambassador Nomura, I called on Postmaster General Frank Walker. After relaying to us similar information, he asked Ambassador Nomura if he was fully aware of the difference between military oil and civilian oil. He appeared to be very happy.

However, the reply,[5] which we received from our government, was a very furious one, almost a reprimand. It read: "The pressing situation of today absolutely cannot be saved with merely such a guarantee as to restore the situation to that which existed prior to the freezing of funds. . . There absolutely is no such time as to continue the talk upon initiation of means to alleviate the situation." It censured us for having presented our plan without prior arrangements as "regrettable in view of the delicate domestic situation" and directed us to submit without fail Plan (B) at our next meeting, stating: "So long as America's acceptance of the above cannot be had, it cannot be helped should the negotiation be ruptured."[6]

In view of the fact that time was pressing, it was unavoidable that the attitude of the government was so rigid. Finally, it was decided to submit Plan (B), appended with the clause that the troops in Southern French Indo-China would be moved to the north, at the next meeting with Secretary of State Hull on the 20th.

Chapter 9

The Deteriorating One Week

On 20 November Plan (B) was submitted. Since the subsequent developments are dwelled on fully in Ambassador Nomura's book, I will refrain from repeating them in a similar form. The primary reasons why America refused to give her consent to Plan (B) were as follows:

1. Discontinuation of aid to Chiang Kai-shek is tantamount to discontinuation of aid to Great Britain. America, in opposing Germany's insatiable armed aggression policy, absolutely cannot accept it.
2. Regarding the transfer of troops in French Indo-China to the north, the transfer of troops in Southern French Indo-China merely to the north would still keep the troops of the other nations concerned, including America, in the Southwest Pacific area.
3. The statements of important government leaders, as usual, advocate the Hitler-styled armed aggrandizement policy. There is none such as would give credence to this peaceful intention of Japan.
4. Japan's furious request for a reply without consideration of the fact that each of the nations concerned, such as Great Britain, the Netherlands and China, must request their respective government for instructions and that America has various domestic reasons given the impression as though it were a demand.

Besides these points, the Americans seemed to have placed considerable concern on the fact that they were receiving continuous reports regarding the strengthening of our troops in the Southwest Pacific area and the negation of a Japan-Siam (Thailand) Alliance, regarded as prelude to an incursion into Siam.

In regard to the first of America's reasons for refusal, the discontinuance of aid to Chiang Kai-shek, since the President had already suggested becoming the "introducer," the result naturally should lead to an armistice between Japan and China. Consequently, I voiced the contention in Washington that it was only proper for Japan to request the discontinuance of aid to Chiang Kai-shek and this, too, was repeated by Foreign Minister Tōgō in Tokyo.[1]

America's contention was that should she take into consideration the instance she will have to act as go-between and make such promise beforehand, she would not be able to act as an impartial "introducer," that if aid is to be discontinued simultaneously with the opening of a negotiation between Japan and China, there would be no particular value in making such a promise now and that aid to Chiang, at any rate, was not as great as reported.

At any rate, various rumors concerning the conclusion of a Japanese-American conciliation were spread following the submission of our Plan (B), and since pro-Chinese views stating "Don't sell China down the river," began to be voiced in various circles as a result, it was not possible for the American Government to ignore such pressure.

In regard to the second point, the transfer of troops in Southern French Indo-China to the north, it was stressed, as instructed by our government, by Ambassador Nomura, as a military man, that it was an extremely important concession from a military point of view, but America would not readily agree to it. It seemed that America's feeling of uneasiness and doubt was greatly intensified through the reports of the strengthening of our troops in the Southwest Pacific area as mentioned previously.

In regard to the statement of Japanese government leaders, it probably referred to the American newspaper correspondents' reports of the speeches of Finance Minister Okinori Kaya and President Kantarō Suzuki of the Planning Board made before the Prefectural Governors convention and the Imperial Rule Assistance Association Central Cooperative Committee's convention held just recently in Tokyo. It may be said that there was a tendency within a group in our country to think that advocacy of a tough attitude was a means to bring about a compromise. After my return to Japan, I was invited to Kinsui in Tsukiji by Mr. Taketora Ogata, editor of the *Asahi Shimbun*, an influential leader of the newspaper circle, and as explained by him on that occasion, the reason may have been that our people, in general, had become accustomed to hearing the use of strong adjectives in manifesting the so-called tough attitude since the Manchurian Incident and thus did not realize the intensity of the expressions.

Furthermore, there appeared to be a custom in our country in the past for cabinet ministers and other responsible men to thoughtlessly read the speeches prepared by their subordinates at various functions. Such customs in some ways contributed to the misunderstanding, and for Americans, who placed emphasis on speeches, it was indeed unfortunate. At the meeting of 22 November Secretary of State Hull went to the extent of saying "properly speaking, even if you were to foresee that war is inevitable, isn't it the proper thing for a statesman to keep trying up to the last moment?"[2]

Of course, there were many considerably strong views in America, too. Many such jingoistic views that Japan will be a push-over in the event of a war appeared in the newspapers. Even Secretary of Navy Knox's speech, which I heard of during my flight over, appeared to have been made an impression in Japan, but it must be recognized that the speeches of responsible Americans, as a rule, were very prudent.

In regard to the fourth point, our apparent demand for a speedy conclusion, Secretary of State Hull flared up somewhat at the meeting of the 22nd at the urgency of Japan's request and explained the need of conferring with other nations, he stated, and "There is a limit to my power. Beyond that, it's impossible." He even stated that in spite of the effort he was making, Japan's feverish insistence for an answer discouraged him.[3]

In reply, an explanation[4] from Tokyo was received to the effect that "For American to call it a demand is a misunderstanding. In view of the fact that our situation is pressing, it is needless to state that our intention is nothing more than a desire for a speedy conciliation." Even the time limit, which had been extended after so much trouble, was attached with a proviso[5] that "arrangements will be made to wait until the completion of not only the signing, but all steps connected with the securing of the promises of Great Britain and the Netherlands through the exchange of official documents" by the 29th. Furthermore, not only did they send this plan for the exchange of documents, but also stipulated the amount of oil required. I fully sympathized with and understood the predicament of the government, which was being pressed by the domestic situation, particularly the army and the navy. If it had been an insignificant government official, it would have been different matter, but a government of a nation standing on the important cross-road of war or peace upon which the fate of the nation was dependent on should have steadfastly maintained a broader point of view and should have had the tact to grasp hold of a chance for peace to the vary last, regardless of the formula.

Nevertheless, it seemed that such political effort and the administrative procedural anxiety for the completion of the documents, for example, were at least handled alike at that time. At any rate, the one week following the submission of Plan (B) was the most important period since my participation in the negotiation; and in the final analysis, it turned out to be the turning point for war or peace.

To that extent, various rumors from various circles were circulated. We heard such news and reports as a conditional agreement of three months duration would be concluded; the Secretary of State had held two discussion with the representatives of Great Britain, the Netherlands, Australia and China, he was discussing solely with the British Ambassador, his recent discussion with the British Ambassador lasted for about an hour, T. V. (Tzu-wen) Soong, together with Ambassador Hu Shih, had called at the White House and left after a 30 minutes discussion, but their attitude was very sullen, and Dorothy Thompson (a leading American woman journalist) had telephoned Secretary of State Hull and warned him not to sell China down the river.

Chapter 10

My Conference with Hull at His Home

Besides the conference with Secretary of State Hull on the 22nd together with Ambassador Nomura, I had called on the Secretary of State alone at his home the day before,[1] the 21st. On this independent call, I had taken along my private plan concerning the Tripartite Alliance. This private plan was an unsigned document in which I, as a signatory of the Tripartite Pact, explained that there was no hidden protocol in the Tripartite Pact, that in the event American should take part in the European war, Japan alone would determine as to whether American had entered the war upon being attacked and that Japan would act independently and not be bound by the interpretations of the other pact members.[2]

It was my plan to show this privately to Secretary of State Hull and sign and submit it to him on the spot if the relationship of Japan and the Tripartite Alliance became clear and the Secretary of State should conclude that it would expedite the Japanese-American negotiation.[3]

The text of this unsigned document was merely the documentation of the last paragraph of the government's instruction[4] concerning the explanation of Plan (B), rejected just the day before. Only there was a parenthesized warning in the interpretation, namely, "the explanation of this clause, however, shall be withheld until the possibility of concluding an agreement becomes apparent." It was fully realized that this warning was made on the fear that the explanation might be used advantageously for propaganda and other purposes should the negotiation fail and it remained in the hands of America. However, there would be no such need for such an explanation should there be a possibility of concluding the negotiation, as suggested in the instruction.[5] I thought that the explanation should be used just then when the success of the negotiation hung in balance. Therefore, I merely took the precaution to leave it unsigned and showed it secretly to Secretary of State Hull.[6]

Upon glancing through the document, Secretary of State Hull asked if he could keep it because he wanted to show it to someone else. When I inquired if that someone was the President, he replied no. Then I asked him if he intended to present it at a cabinet meeting, he again replied no. As to who this individual was it was not revealed, but I imagine it might have been Secretary of Navy Knox. At any rate, I left the document unsigned in the hands of Secretary of State Hull.[7]

The independent meeting lasted for about 30 minutes.[8] His attitude was very friendly and he even jokingly remarked, "Since you have come from afar, I ordinarily, would invite you to dinner or to play a game of golf, but we are quite busy and I have found that golfing takes up too much time and does not mix well with state affairs." Even in regard to the question of the Tripartite Alliance, he stated that the remark made during the conference with the President on the 17th that the Tripartite Alliance would be outshone should a general Pacific area agreement be concluded was a very telling remark. Thus, stating that his cooperation with the Japanese delegate at the 1933 London Economic Conference was one of his pleasant memories, he made such remarks as it was only proper for Japan to be the leader in East Asia so long as she remained peaceful; that the phrase East Asia Co-Prosperity Sphere was very crude as an explanation, but understandable as an idea and that he hoped for the reappearance of such a period as that of the Russo-Japanese war when Japan and America held positions of leadership, in East Asia and the western hemisphere, respectively, and their relations were amicable and cooperative. He revealed his innermost thought, stating that he was fully aware of the fact that Ambassador Nomura and I were earnestly striving for peace, but could not do as we pleased because of the restraint of the militarists behind us. Even in America, Secretary Hull could not do things as he wanted because of politicians.

On this day, Secretary of State Hull appeared to have had a slight cold and when I shook his hand on parting, I felt it to be feverish. I parted with the remark that he take care of his health.[9] Thus, while the Secretary of State was working very hard under such circumstances, we, being pressed by the time limit and the demands of our government, were forced to request repeatedly for America's reply. Consequently, we fully understood the Secretary of State's frame of mind when he expressed his dissatisfaction during the conference held with Ambassador Nomura and myself on the following day, the 22nd.

Chapter 11
Hull's Fatal Note

Secretary of State Hull's attitude, which had been friendly and cheerful until the conference of 26 November, appeared to have changed suddenly. I came to think of it later, but it was because of an important reason.

Dispatch #726 from Togo to Nomura was sent on the day of my departure, 5 November. This was one of the reasons for the misunderstanding that I had come to America with the knowledge that a final ultimatum would be submitted. That this message had been intercepted by America has been explained at the beginning of this book. Furthermore, this intercepted message had been completely mistranslated and it appears as if the translation was completed and shown to the Secretary of State on about the 22nd. Vice-Minister of Foreign Affairs Haruhiko Nishi, for example, stated that the administrative section considers the interception of this message as one of the important causes of the war.

The message in question was the instruction from Tokyo concerning Plan (A), which was one of our final plans. Although the original message and as its beginning the phrase "as a final conciliatory plan," America's intercepted message read "as a final revised ultimatum." The original message also listed the substance of the plan as (1), (2), and (3) and explained, as a proviso, that it was not desired to have the four principles (Secretary of State Hull's claims) included within the formally agreed matters in any shape or form, but the four of the our principles was listed as (4) and translated as "(4) As a matter of principle we are anxious to avoid having this inserted in the draft of the formal proposal." Therefore, the interpretation could not help but be "even if an agreement should be reached on the various matters of (1), (2) and (3), we would like to avoid having them be made formal." Consequently, the reason for the negotiation became lost and the proposal became an extreme case of making a complete fool of the individuals concerned. It is only logical that America, including Secretary of State Hull, became offended upon reading this mistranslation and reached the conclusion that Japan possessed no sincerity. I cannot help but assert that this is the worst mishap of misreading and misinterpretation.

I have not yet read Secretary of State Hull's book, but I, in ill-health, have heard that the Secretary of State, in his book, attacks me personally on the ground that I was already aware of this message at the time of my departure from Tokyo. I believe that this probably is based on this grossly mistranslated message.[1]

The second message pertaining to the four principles of America then was translated into English, as follows:

1. This proposal is our revised ultimatum made as a result of our attempt to meet, in so far as possible, the wishes of the Americans, clarified as a result of negotiation based on our proposals of September 25. We have toned down our insistences as follows:
   (1)-(2) Omitted
   (4) As a matter of principle we are anxious to avoid having this inserted in the draft of the formal proposal reached between Japan and the United States (whether it is called an understanding, proposal, or some other sort of a statement).

According to the Japanese text of the original message, which became the substance of the code, the fourth paragraph, mentioned above, was as follows:

Moreover, in regard to the four principles, make every effort to avoid having them included within the matters formally agreed between Japan and the United States (whether it be an understanding or any other type of statement. (Note)

Note: On the back of the paper upon which Kumaichi Yamamoto, who was then head of the American Affairs Bureau under the Vice-Minister of Foreign Affairs, wrote in pencil the following:

"Since there are passages in Tōgō's explanation being drafted at present by Mr. Blakely (Tōgō's Attorney) making a comparatively detailed study of this matter, I'll let you see it when I receive a copy." Yamamoto, To Ambassador Kurusu

Chapter 12

Negotiation Falls into a Tight Spot

I seem to continuously disagree, but I would like to state at the beginning that the influence of the navy was very strong within America at that time. One of the reasons may have been due to the fact that President Roosevelt was pro-navy. Ambassador Nomura and the president became acquainted with each other when Ambassador Nomura had served as naval attaché at the Embassy and the president was Assistant Secretary of the Navy during World War I.

This happened when Prosecutor Keenan had returned to Japan from his trip to America and just before the discovery of the mistranslation of the coded message. The prosecutor told me that he was asked by those close to the president in Washington why MacArthur's headquarters had not arrested Kurusu. Gen. MacArthur reportedly stated that in as much as the American people are regarded as decent people, that action is inconceivable.

Then, the prosecution, intending to use me as a witness, inquired if I had thought Hull's note of 26 November was the final ultimatum. To this, I replied that I didn't consider it to be a final ultimatum, but it could have been considered as such under the circumstance at the time. It seems that the prosecution was afraid that I would be exploited by the defense and did not use me as a witness. At any rate, as I would not make a hasty decision on anything, the prosecutor appeared to have been greatly dissatisfied on this point.

Thus, the unforgettable 26th November came, and Ambassador Nomura and I conferred[1] with the Secretary of State at 4:45 p.m. and received a note[2], dated that day, which today has become a famous historical document.

On the margin at the top, it read "Tentative and without commitment" and they explained that it was a plan, but from its content, we realized that America had not conceded even a step from her past contentions. Not only that, but there were many points logically indicating that the negotiation had returned completely to its beginning. In reply to Plan (B), our final plan, in particular, it according to the oral statement[3] exchanged simultaneously then, stated, "The Government of the United States of America believes that the adoption of such a plan will contribute to the ultimate aim of preserving peace in the Pacific area, based on law, order, and righteousness, and suggests that further efforts be made to settle the difference of opinion between both countries concerning the practical application of the already mentioned basic principles." In other words, it suggested further discussions such as Plan (B) were not acceptable. Consequently, since we had been instructed, as mentioned previously, at the time of the submission of Plan (B) that "it cannot be helped if the negotiation should be ruptured so long as America's acceptance cannot be had regarding the above," and in view of the fact that we had a time limit requiring the signing of the agreement by the 29th, our disappointment was very great.

In regard to the details of the meeting of the 26th, I will leave it to Ambassador Nomura's book. However, the principal point of the explanation made by me during this discussion was this. In regard to the paragraph pertaining to the conclusion of a multilateral non-aggression pact (clause 2 of the note), I explained that in view of the bitter experiences suffered since the Washington Conference, which I had repeatedly mentioned in the past discussions, to order us to reactivate a machinery similar to the Nine Power Pact would be tantamount to ordering us to completely ignore the Sino-Japanese incident of the past four years. To this, no strong refutation was made by Secretary of State Hull. I further explained that both items, the total withdrawal of our land, sea and air force and our police strength (Section 2-(3) of the note) and the supporting of no other government than Chungking (Section 2-(4) of the note), were impossible proposals, and that just as America cannot sell the Chiang regime down the river, so cannot Japan sell the Nanking government down the river. In reply, he countered that there was no other alternative but to regard the Nanking government as absolutely lacking in power to govern China. In regard to the withdrawal of our troops and other forces, he merely replied that it did not necessarily mean that they were demanding its immediate realization but failed to make any explanation or demand in detail on both matters. His whole attitude appeared to indicate that to argue was practically useless, leaving us with no one to turn to.

According to the diary of Secretary of War Stimson, published in the report of the Army Board of Inquiry and the Navy Board of Inquiry on the Pearl Harbor question, (pages 154-156 of the *Japan Times* publication), the Secretary of State told the Secretary of War on the morning of 26 November that it had been practically decided not to submit the three months conditional agreement shown to the Secretaries of the Navy and the War the day before and to "kick the whole thing over." Furthermore, in a telephone conversation with the Secretary of War on the morning of the 27th, the Secretary of State reportedly stated, "I have washed my hand off it, and it is in the hands of you and Knox, the Army and Navy." The Secretary of State must have passed the note to us in that same frame of mind when we met in the afternoon of the 26th.

At the end of the discussion, I stated that since we strongly doubted whether it would be the proper action for us, who sincerely hoped for the adjustment of the relations between Japan and America, to relay this note, as is, to our government. We would like to decide after having further reading and careful discussion, and when Ambassador Nomura inquired if it meant that America had no room for other consideration besides this plan, Secretary of State Hull replied that it, after all, was a plan.[4]

In as much as the president had stated, "There is no last words among friends," Ambassador Nomura repeated his request for an appointment to talk with the President once more. To this, the Secretary of State appeared not to be in the mood for it, but finally agreed.

Thus did we accept America's note of 26 November. Since the difference of opinion between Japan and America was too great, the possibility of America's acceptance of our claims within the time limit specified by our government became absolutely nil. What attitude would our government assume? This inevitably became our object of great concern.

We thought that it would be a grave matter if our government should suddenly undertake an unrestrained action without any manifestation of her intention to break off the negotiation, in particular. Although we had pressed America for a speedy settlement of the negotiation, according to the instructions of our government, we had never at any time made any final ultimatum-like gesture. We thus immediately sent a cable,[5] stating that since the President had said, "There is no last words among friends," and they, in fact, were negotiating and consulting with the other nations concerned, they will criticize us and propagandize to the world that we had prolonged the discussion until the completion of our military preparation and had undertaken the action at our convenience should we undertake an unrestrained action without any warning. Although there may be military reasons, we would like our government to clearly indicate the breaking off of the negotiation at her own discretion in such an event either through a notification to the American Ambassador in Tokyo or a statement to the world and to secretly inform us simultaneously.

This cable was sent on the eve of the final meeting with the President.

Chapter 13

Our Second Meeting with the President

Our meeting[1] with the President was held on 27 November amidst such an oppressive atmosphere. The previous meeting, that is, the meeting of the 17th, was held in the official reception room of the White House, but this was held in a room appearing to be the office of the President. Of course, the Secretary of State was present.[2]

The situation then was not only pressing to me, for according to the literature made public since the end of the war, the President, too, appeared to have been fully cognizant of the seriousness of the situation. In fact, according to the Stimson diary, which I mentioned before, the President, in a meeting with the Secretaries of State, War and Navy, the Chief of Staff and the Chief of Naval Operations at the White House on 25 November, had reportedly stated that Japan might execute a surprise attack next Monday (1 December). In spite of this, the attitude of the President toward us was suave and graceful and cheerful.

After we had taken our seats and Ambassador Nomura had accepted a cigarette offered by the President, the President personally lit a match and attempted to light the cigarette, but Ambassador Nomura, having only one good eye, could not bring the point of his cigarette to the light extended by the President. The President laughed and extended his hand farther to light the cigarette.[3] The president then explained that he usually took his vacation and went to the country for a rest at this time of the year, but because of Envoy Kurusu's visit and the problems caused by John L. Lewis of the coal miners' union this year, he has not been able to vacation as yet. Therefore, I expressed my apologies and laughingly inquired as to who caused him the greater trouble, Lewis or I, the president burst out in laughing and replied Lewis, of course. Consequently, the meeting was begun ostensibly in an extremely amicable atmosphere.

The president, then, pointed out that Japan and America had suffered together as allies during the last World War because Germany was not able to understand the psychology of the other nations. I wonder if the president wanted to make us recall the friendly Japanese-American relations that existed during the last World War through this statement and, at the same time, make the group in Japan reconsider their attitude by referring to the attitude of Germany of the past. Continuing further, he explained that he was happy to hear that there have been some peace advocates in Japan who have been exerting their efforts ever since the beginning of the negotiation and that he still had great hopes of Japan and America arriving at a peaceful settlement. Therefore, Ambassador Nomura began with the remark that he was in agreement with the remarks of the president but that the latest American proposal had caused Japan to become disillusioned.

In reply, the president stated that he, too, was disappointed that the situation had come to such a pass, but that he had felt a chill creep over him the first time several months after the beginning of the negotiation when Japanese troops advanced into Southern French Indo-China, and the recent reports made him fear he would again feel a chill creep over him.[4]

In all probability, the President must have been receiving in rapid succession from the American authorities stationed along the coast of French Indo-China and China reports of the movement of our land and sea forces, the unloading of various weapons and the movements of our transports.[5] The situation wherein the negotiation would become much more difficult as the deployment of our strength became known was gradually becoming a reality, just as Foreign Minister Tōgō had feared at the time of my departure from Tokyo.

Particularly, just about the time when this discussion was held, rumors circulated that Japan was conducting an important negotiation with Thailand. We imagined that the president worried about losing face should such a thing as Thai-Japan military agreement be concluded and our troops moved into Thailand just as negotiations between Japan and America were continuing. Hence, the American government's distrust of our militarists had already increased to this extent.

The president further explained that as stated by Envoy Kurusu recently, he was fully aware that the frame of mind of the Japanese people, who had suffered four years of war, could not be measured by the standard of peaceful America, but the fact that there had been no peaceful statements from the leaders of Japan during the discussions between the Secretary of State and us had made this negotiation very difficult. He stated that even the plan to develop the situation through a conditional agreement, in the final analysis, would be of no use if we did not agree on the basic principles pertaining to the disposition of the Japanese-American relations. He explained that even in his discussion at sea with Prime Minister Churchill, for example, the fundamental policies of both were in agreement and the matters to be discussed were known beforehand.

However, such was possible between nations such as America and Great Britain, where the political situation was normal, but it must be said that it, regrettably, was an impossibility for Japan, whose political situation had been extremely abnormal following such incidents as the May 15 (1932) and the February 26 (1936) incident.[6]

I once heard a parable from Lord Keeper of the Privy Seal Kido pertaining to the developments preventing the materialization of the discussion at sea between Konoye and Roosevelt. The story went like this. Japan invites America upstairs to take in a beautiful view, but America wants to know beforehand what kind of view it is. Japan insists that America would find out if she would go upstairs. It went on like this until nothing was accomplished. However, America may have been afraid that the ladder would be taken away if she went upstairs. At any rate, it must be said that it was practically impossible to explain this abnormal situation of Japan to the satisfaction of foreigners without discrediting Japan.

As the conversations continued, a discussion on China's economy was held between Secretary of State Hull and myself. When Secretary of State Hull stated that Japan not infrequently protected the sale of morphine, I cited the case of carpet-bagging during the time of the American Civil War.[7] Then, when we referred to the president's proposal to act as "introducer," the president only replied that he still had the idea, but did not reveal the details.

Finally, the conference ended with Ambassador Nomura, relying on his friendship of thirty years with the president, appealing to him to break the deadlock with his statement. In other words, with this discussion our effort to make America reconsider and bring about a change in the deadlock ended in a complete failure.[8]

The negotiation now was in a practically hopeless situation. The Secretary of State, who had been silent to the newspapers and others concerning the negotiation in the past, voluntarily made a public statement concerning the meeting, of the 26th. Responding to this, the newspapers, with such headlines as "Hull Hands Peace Plan to Japan" and "American Rejects Second Munich Plan," emphasized such points of Secretary of State Hull's so-called four basic principles against which no one could raise an objection as abstract arguments and wrote that it was up to Japan whether to accept America's proposal, but it was solely Japan's responsibility as to whether there would be war or peace.[9]

Chapter 14

Premier Tōjō's Speech to Expel America and Great Britain

The American atmosphere centering around the note of 26 November, in general, was as mentioned in the preceding chapter, but Japan's reaction became clear through the government's dispatch[1] of 26 November. This dispatch was a reply to our message in which we had taken the trouble to report the gist of the note immediately following its receipt.

The government's dispatch explained that it regarded America's note as "surprising and regrettable" and instructed us that Japan absolutely cannot consider this note as an overture, that there was no alternative but to submit to them the "Imperial government's opinion" to be wired in two or three days and in reality to break off the negotiation. Tokyo was anxious "to avoid giving the impression that the negotiation had been broken off" to the other party, but we were to explain to the American government that we had no knowledge of the government's view in as much as we were still waiting for the instruction. We should give as our opinion that in spite of the fact that Japan had been making just claims in the past and had manifested a conciliatory attitude even to the extent of making unbearable sacrifices often for the sake of peace in the Pacific, in particular, America had made no response and had now presented this new plan to make the conclusion of the negotiation impossible.

Then, on the 30th, we were instructed to present the following points[2] orally once more;

"It is difficult for the Imperial government to understand that the American government has considered our new proposal, based on our righteous position and formulated after having fully considered the past claims of both, as impossible to regard as a basis for discussion and had presented the new plan of the 26th, which ignores the realities of East Asia and contains not only a few points pertaining to the authority of the Imperial government, and her ever-changing attitude regarding the China problem, for example, makes the Imperial government suspect the nature of her basic aims, which she has been formulating during the negotiation of the past seven months."

Consequently, we presented this to the Secretary of State on 1 December.[3] However, just before this, Premier Tōjō's American and British expulsion speech was greatly played up in the American newspapers on 30 November. Above all, the part claiming that British and American exploitation of the Asiatic races "should be exterminated with vengeance" was given larger publicity.

Since the Prime Minister had clamored for the expulsion of the opposing country in which not one, but two of this ambassadors were busily engaged in a negotiation, it was not unreasonable for the repercussion it caused within the various quarters of America to have been so strong as to be beyond the imagination of the people in Japan.

According to the reports of the American newspapers then, Secretary of State Hull telephoned and reported it immediately to the President, who was resting at Warm Springs. Cutting short his rest, the president immediately left Warm Springs that afternoon and returned to Washington on the morning of the 1st. When we called on the Secretary of State on 1 December, for example, newspapermen as well as individuals believed to be employees of the State Department were gathered along the hallways and passages, whispering to each other. Everything gave the appearance of something important about to happen.

According to the explanation[4] of our government given in reply to our wire[5] hastily inquiring about the actual facts concerning the speech, the speech in question had been written by the General Affairs Office of the Rising Asia Federation. It was to be the Premier's congratulatory speech for the celebration commemorating the first anniversary of the signing of the Sino-Japanese Basic Agreement, sponsored by the Rising Asia Federation on 30 November. As the celebration was to fall on Sunday, a member of the General Affairs office had given copies of the speech to the newspaper reporters on the night of 29th. The reply further stated: "The premier, himself, has made no speech on the 30th and the government, including the premier, was completely unaware of the manuscript." We on the spot indeed could not help but be dumbfounded.

Moreover, according to the government's explanation, the clause in question was "For the honor and pride of mankind we must purge the sort of practice from East Asia with vengeance."[6] No matter how we tried to explain, it was, in other words, water under the bridge. Since several days earlier the speeches of Cabinet members Okinori Kaya and Teiichi

Suzuki had been reported as clamoring for the ousting of Great Britain and America and now the Premier himself had been reported as demanding for the purging of Great Britain and America, Americans were greatly shocked.

The 1 December meeting[7] with Secretary of State was held at the Department of State under such an extremely tense atmosphere. As at the very outset the Secretary of State touched upon the Premier's speech with a grave expression, I explained that I believed the Premier's speech probably had been twisted and exaggerated, stating that if only a certain portion and not the complete text of anyone's speech is given, the real intention of the talker could be misinterpreted into something with an entirely different meaning. In the meantime, the Secretary of State gradually calmed down and repeated, as usual, that it was regrettable that he had heard no statement supporting the negotiation and contributing toward a change in the situation from responsible leaders of Japan ever since the beginning of the negotiation.[8] He stated that because of this silence, there had been considerable criticism within the country and that he was in a very embarrassing position.

Then, the Secretary of State revealed that he was receiving in rapid succession from the American authorities on the spot reports concerning the latest deployment of our troops in the Southwest Pacific area. He explained that we would be able to fully understand how America felt today if our positions were reversed and the Japanese army and navy were placed in a similar position. Although Japan has repeatedly explained that she had no aggressive intentions, Japan, from America's point of view, could be interpreted as assisting Hitler so that America and the other nations concerned must divide their respective military strength and concentrate them in the said area. No matter how desirous of a compromise America might be, her hands were completely tied in view of the speeches of the leaders of Japan today.

As the close of the meeting, I stated that the motto "Don't sell China down the river" was prevalent in America, but would not Japan and America be selling themselves down the river if they should eventually go to war against each other because of the China question.[9] In reply the Secretary of State nodded, but only repeated that in view of the present situation, he wanted Japan to open the way for a fresh development through the improvement of her speeches.

Thus, the government ordered time limit was already over by one day even from Premier Tōjō's personal instruction of "by the end of November."

Chapter 15

Plan for the Exchange of Messages between the Heads of State

Until the situation came to such a pass, we, of course, had considered a number of plans for breaking the deadlock, and it may be stated with due reverence that one of the plans was to trouble the Emperor.

At the time of the resignation of the Third Konoye Cabinet, I had heard that there was a plan by some Americans to have the President send a cable to the emperor to prevent the resignation of the Konoye Cabinet. Even after my arrival in Washington, I heard from Secretary Terasaki of the Embassy that the Rev. Stanley Jones, an influential man in the Christian circles of America, had a plan to urge the President into sending a wire to the Emperor as a means of breaking the deadlock in the Japanese-American negotiation and that he was incessantly campaigning for it. Besides, I had heard from another source that Senator Elbert Thomas of Utah had a similar idea. The date of the time limit was gradually drawing near with practically no hope of American accepting Plan (B). Moreover, even our government had started that "it cannot be helped if the negotiation should be broken off" should plan (B) not be accepted. Placing my hope on these reports and thinking that there was no way to break the deadlock other than an exchange of telegrams between the two heads of the state, I wrote the following dispatch[1] on 26 November;

"As indicated in my successive wire, there is no hope for the acceptance of Plan (B) in its entirety. On the other hand, with the time drawing near, I am overwhelmed with shame at my helplessness in as much as there is no other alternative but to break off the negotiation if it proceeds as is, although regrettable. I am filled with trepidation to make this suggestion, but the only means of breaking the deadlock at this time is to have President Roosevelt send a wire to the Emperor expressing his desire for Japanese-American cooperation for the preservation of peace in the Pacific (will await your wishes and negotiation as best as I can) and to have the Emperor reply to this, thus, completely changing the atmosphere and, at the same time, obtaining an extension of a little more time. Taking into consideration the possibility that Great Britain and America may undertake a protective occupation of the Netherlands East Indies and French Indo-China, I believe it best that we take the initiative and propose the creation of neutral area, including the Netherlands East Indies, French Indo-China and Thailand (In September of this year, President Roosevelt, as you know, proposed the neutrality of French Indo-China and Thailand).[2] Although there is an observation that breaking off the negotiation at this time does not necessarily mean a Japanese-American war, it is anticipated that Great Britain and America will move into the Netherlands East Indies and French Indo-China following the rupture of the negotiation and ultimately our attack will make inevitable a clash with Great Britain and the Netherlands. In the event, it is very doubtful as to whether Germany will execute her obligation as stipulated in Article 3, and there will be no choice but to postpone the settlement of Sino-Japanese incident at least until the end of the current world war. As this probably will be my last opinion to be presented, I hope that you will show this at least to the Lord Keeper of the Privy Seal Kido and send me a reply immediately."[3]

At first, I had intended to send this dispatch entirely as my own. This was because I thought that this was a very important matter, that it would be a very serious blunder if the President's consent could not be obtained when the time came for the American group to ask the President to send the wire or if the text of the President's wire should not be exactly as I desired after our government had sounded out the wishes of the Emperor and obtained his consent. I wanted to avoid making Ambassador Nomura share the responsibility in such an event. However, as Ambassador Nomura stubbornly insisted on sharing the responsibility, it was finally sent out under our joint signature.

The reason I listed the possibility of the protective occupation of the Netherlands East Indies and French Indo-China by America was that I had already known through the American government's public statement on November 24 that America, after having conferred with the Netherlands government in Washington, had Dutch Guiana already placed under protective occupation to protect the aluminum resources and that Brazil had also taken part in the move.

However, the Foreign Minister's reply to this dispatch was that he had consulted with the Lord Keeper of the Privy Seal Kido and he had said that it was not the time to take such action.[4] However, as everyone knows, the President finally did send a message addressed to the Emperor about ten days later on 6 December.[5] This is what I heard directly from Premier Tōjō at a luncheon to which Ambassador Nomura and I were invited upon our return to Japan aboard the exchange ship. It would have been difficult to start the war had the President's message of 6 December arrived several days earlier and if the American note of 26 November had been a bit more conciliatory. Moreover, it was not several days, but about ten days earlier that I had proposed the exchange of messages between the two heads of the state.

This, too, I heard after my return to Japan. Foreign Minister Tōgō stated that our request for an exchange of message was not timely from the standpoint of the situation at that moment. When Ambassador Nomura and I were invited to dinner at the home of the Lord Keeper of the Privy Seal at Toriizaka, Azabu, Marquis Kido revealed his predicament of that time, stating "It's embarrassing because the Americans seem to think that anything can be done by troubling the Emperor."

Later on 1 December, we again made another suggestion[6] to our government. We suggested that although there was the experience of the failure of the Konoye-Roosevelt talk to materialize, how would it be to propose, as our plan, the idea of having Premier Konoye or Viscount Ishii from Japan meet with Vice-President Henry Wallace or Harry Hopkins, one of President Roosevelt's "Brain-trusters," from America to devise a final plan for the breaking of the deadlock. This, too, was not approved by our government.

Now, another problem I could hardly forget was our relations with another power, particularly Great Britain. The plan to seek for the assistance of Great Britain, upon which I had placed some hope at the time of my departure from Tokyo, had become practically hopeless because of Prime Minister Churchill's speech, which I became cognizant of during my stay on Midway where the plane had made an emergency landing. However, soon after my arrival in Washington, Ambassador Nomura suggested that we, at any rate, might call on British Ambassador Lord Halifax in the sense of paying a courtesy call on the British Ambassador since I had newly arrived in America.[7] As I had once met Lord Halifax, although casually, at a banquet at the Japanese Embassy in London, I agreed with the opinion of Ambassador Nomura. We had a call put through to the British Embassy and relayed our intention, but we were only told that the British Ambassador was travelling in Philadelphia and never heard from him later.

Later, on 30 November, Australian Minister Richard Casey called on me at our Embassy.[8] He stated that he believed the situation had become considerably pressing by Hull's note of the 26 November and that I should meet with Ambassador Halifax as he, personally, would intercede. As Ambassador Nomura happened to come into the reception room during the conversation, we, three, made further arrangements.[9] Not long after he had left, Casey telephoned to inform us that the matter of meeting with the British Ambassador be dropped. It probably was because he was not able to obtain the consent of the British Ambassador.[10] We believed that Ambassador Halifax, who was foreign minister when I was arriving in Europe, probably knew of the details of my attempt to readjust the Anglo-Japanese relations while in Europe and my ultimate failure to obtain the consent of our government.[11]

We naturally considered the scheme of working from the side toward the Americans and also had received instructions from our government in regard to this. It is needless to state that it is, generally speaking, necessary to be very careful in obtaining lateral assistance without giving the other party an unpleasant feeling and to conduct such scheme seemingly naturally and effectively, a considerably wide and profound friendship and a sufficient extension of time are necessary. But what could we do? As far as I know, the friendly relations of our Embassy so painstakingly built up by our successive ambassadors appeared to have practically vanished with the aggravation of the Japanese-American relations.

In fact, the situation was such that that the Embassy could not hold a single tea party in spite of the fact that I had come to Washington from afar. Besides, of the Americans with whom I had struck up friendship at various places throughout the world and even the diplomats and others who were supposed to be living in Washington, practically all of them had left the State Department and only those not close to the regime of that time were numerous. Even from the standpoint of sufficiency of time, I was pressed with work from the day of my arrival and had no time to do other things. For example, even the replies to the letters received daily from numerous friends and strangers, they were practically handled by Secretary Yuuki. The condition was such that even the replies to the letters from old friends were delayed at times, resulting in complaints over the telephone. Hence, there was practically no time to work on the scheme of lateral assistance.

Such was the case that it was even very rare for me to have my meals outside of the Embassy. I was invited once for dinner by the Brazilian Ambassador and his wife with whom I was on friendly terms as a result of having been colleagues while in Japan and Belgium, once for dinner by former Acting American Minister Ferdinand Mayer with whom I had been intimate while serving in South America, and once for luncheon by former American Ambassador Joseph E. Davies with whom I had been friendly while serving in Europe.

As friends, these individuals sympathized with me concerning my mission, but had no connection with our lateral assistance scheme. I merely had the chance to talk with them socially. Former American Ambassador Davies, for example, was a friend of the President and also friendly with Secretary of State Hull, but he had been a pessimist concerning the future of Japanese-American relations form the time I met him in Washington on my way back from Germany.

On this occasion, he had taken the trouble to return to his home in Washington from New York and had invited me to lunch with only his wife and himself, and he had reminiscently wondered if American and Japan, after all, were not to become technical enemies.[12] Davies probably had already surmised the possibility of abrogation of relations between Japan and America as a result of our country's incursion into the Malay Peninsula and Thailand. It appears that there were not a few who had the same view as he that it would be unlikely for our country, weakened by the Sino-Japanese incident of over four years, to declare war against America. However, having heard sometime later that Davies had done much for my sake in Washington when the International Military Tribunal for the Far East was finally convened after the war, I cannot help but be thankful for his kindness.

Chapter 16

The "If" Lurking behind History

There were several Americans whom I felt I would like to meet immediately after the war. All of them were individuals who had assisted me directly or indirectly in Washington. One was Bishop James E. Walsh of the Catholic Church and the other was Dr. Stanley Jones of the Protestant Church.[1] These two Christian leaders visited Japan after the war, one following on the heels of the other, but when Bishop Walsh came to Japan, I lost the chance to meet him as I was living in Karuizawa.

Bishop Walsh is a man who could be called the father of the Japanese American negotiation.[2] When the relations of both countries became extremely strained and the governments of Japan and America had practically given up hope, he, burning with the desire for the preservation of peace, unofficially interceded between the two countries.

In our country, Premier Konoye was finally moved and this opened the way for the beginning of the Japanese-American negotiation. Not only that, he sent his able and experienced man named Father James M. Drought, in whom he had complete confidence, to be in constant touch with our Embassy. As a result, the plan of 16 April, which was a private plan of the Americans, but which, I believe, afforded the best opportunity for a successful Japanese-American negotiation. There was no objection, in general, to this plan from our government and the militaries and even former Premier Reijirō Wakatsuki, who saw this plan, reportedly shed tears of happiness. However, even that plan ended in failure when the consent of Foreign Minister Matsuoka, who had just returned from Germany, could not be obtained.[3]

In spite of this great setback, Bishop Walsh steadfastly continued to assist us even after I arrived in America. He, together with Father Drought, appeared almost daily at the Embassy to help us. It, of course, was an attempt to temporarily alleviate the atmosphere, but he was very cooperative in the attempt to find a plan that would delay the final deterioration of the situation to the last moment.

This, too, was not accepted because of our militarists' useless fear of lowering their dignity and with their attachment of provision completely nullifying the significance and aim of the plan, it ended in failure, leading to the final breakdown of the situation.

Every attempt thus ended in failure, but I believe our country should not forget forever the efforts of Bishop Walsh and Father Drought, who has since passed away.

As I had lost my chance to meet Bishop Walsh, I was very restless for fear that I might miss the opportunity again when the visit of Dr. Stanley Jones, the mediator of President Roosevelt's friendly telegram, was made public.[4]

As I had difficulty in walking and could not get on a tram, I could not pay him a call, although I had heard that he was registered at Teikoku Hotel. Thinking that it would be too discourteous to ask him to come and that very few people knew of my temporary home, I gave up all hope of the possibility of the Doctor obtaining my address by accident and taking the trouble to call on me. However, while the Doctor was travelling in Kyushu, it became accidently known to a member of the *Nishi-Nippon Shimbun* that the Doctor was desirous of meeting and talking with me. My friend, Kiyoshi Komatsu, who was there on a lecture tour of Kyushu, heard of this wish and gave my address to the Doctor, and as soon as he returned to Tokyo, the Doctor took the trouble to call on me.

I was again able to see the kindly countenance of the Doctor, to whom I had entrusted such an important matter, but whom I was unable to see because of the war. Making every effort to restrain my feeling, which has become rather irritable since my sickness, I told him how encouraging it was to me, who had been criticized as "liar" by the great majority of Americans, that he had taken the trouble to thank us by letter for our efforts toward the attainment of peace just prior to our departure aboard the exchange ship, and I thanked him for this kindness.[5]

In response, the Doctor related in detail the action he took immediately after I had appealed for the initiation of the plan for the exchanging of messages between the heads of state through Hidenari Terasaki, the 1st Secretary of the Embassy then, and how he strove to persuade President Roosevelt, and stated that he had an idea that we probably were risking our lives in requesting the execution of the plan. What he meant was that our thought must have been that it couldn't be helped if we were killed should the plan leak out to the militarists and the rightists.

Then, replying to the inquiries of the Doctor, I related my impressions on the progress of the democratization of Japan and expressed my humble opinion pertaining to the role to be played by Christianity during the interim. The Doctor agreed with me in regard to this, and expressing the hope that I would be baptized by the time of his next visit to Japan, he left after giving a short prayer for my sake.

Should my health recover and I am able to attend church without causing too much trouble to others, I thought that I would like to be baptized by the Doctor himself on his next visit to Japan.

What I thought of again upon receiving the visit of the Doctor was my appeal for the assistance of the Doctor and for what reason and by whom was the telegram of the message exchange plan, which was wired to Japan, prevented from reaching the Emperor. In other words, this, too, will remain forever as an "if" hiding in the back of history.

Chapter 17

The Kindness of Baruch

After the war, there were inquiries from an AP correspondent that there reportedly were some Americans who had assisted us and if their identity could be revealed. What he meant was that there must have been such individuals and who were they? Leaving aside those who had come out and identified themselves, I, afraid of causing embarrassment, have maintained complete silence, but today, I believe there is no such necessity.[1]

This happened on 26 November when the negotiation was actually in its final stage. There was a man named Raoul Desvernine, who was the legal advisor of the New York branch of Mitsui Bureau. At this time, he was a complete stranger to me, but he urged me to meet Bernard M. Baruch, a leading figure in the political and financial circles of America, and agreed to arrange the opportunity for the meeting himself.[2]

Baruch is a well-known man, who was President Woodrow Wilson's right hand man during World War I. As head of the War Industry Board, he established the war footing of American industry, and directing it freely, he showed its strength to the world. He was 71 years of age in 1941 and was famous throughout the world. He was in close touch with President Roosevelt, too.

Those who know are aware of his secret power even today. When Prime Minister Winston Churchill visited Washington in 1952, he reportedly stayed at Baruch's home.

There is a hotel called New Willard Hotel in Washington, I was able to meet and talk with Baruch on 30 November in Desvernine's room in this hotel.[3] That the matter had been worked to this extent was due to none other than the efforts of Finance Officer Tsutomu Nishiyama.

I explained the detail of the negotiation as requested by Baruch and sought his assistance. Baruch stated very sincerely as follows: "I have seen Hull's note of 26 November, and it certainly has become a very difficult situation. As it is, there'll be a war, and if war occurs, it is definitely known that Japan has no chance of winning. Even if America wins, it'll mean nothing. Something must be done to straighten out the negotiation and prevent war."

I then replied that since there was no alternative with matters having come to such a state, I would like to have the negotiation straightened out through the political powers of the two heads of state and was hoping that President Roosevelt would send a message to the Emperor. On the other hand, I explained that I was obtaining the help of Dr. Stanley Jones.

Baruch asked what I intended to do after the exchange of messages between the two heads of state and continued as follows:

President Roosevelt made a speech to the effect that he will make America the arsenal of democracy. He is increasing expenditures tremendously, but this cannot be done indefinitely. Sure, we can take out any amount of dollars, but we cannot get steel and oil from dollars. It is a known fact that materials are needed for war. It certainly has become a very difficult situation. I cannot understand the reason why America should risk such a danger and fight against Japan. I find it difficult to understand what America's intention is to finish off Japan. I, personally, don't like present Japan and Germany too much, but I believe we should utilize Japan in the Far East and Germany in Europe in order to realize the world policy America aims for. It would be terrible to destroy Germany and Japan.

He further continued as follows:

To begin with, I know too well the motive for the Japanese militarists' show of Dutch courage and menacing air. The Japanese militarists are nervous as they have become aware of their real strength through the Nomonhan incident.[4] They undoubtedly are making a show of their Dutch courage for nothing, while fretting with the uneasiness brought about by their inferiority complex. Consequently, the Japanese militarists will undoubtedly settle down and think clearly should they be given strength through the promotion of Japan's industry and the expansion of her productive power. If President Roosevelt wants to make America the arsenal of the democratic nations, he should actively assist Japan's industry. I think he should actively utilize it. I believe there isn't a better policy than this for America and for Japan. I may sound like talking too loosely, but how about an investment of $1,000,000,000?[5]

It was a sound argument impregnated with sincerity. I was profoundly moved by the sincere attitude and far-sightedness of this gentleman and earnestly appealed for his assistance. Exactly as he had promised me, Baruch met the President with this idea.

On 3 December, Baruch had lunch and discussed the matter with the President. Stating that he had good results, Baruch asked me if I liked fishing and related the following parable: When a cod-fish sees a bait, it will stay away a while as through it has not seen it and look the situation over. Then, all of a sudden, it'll take hold of it. The President has a similar habit. Since my talk had a definite effect, we promised to meet again on 10 December and parted.

Therefore, I had Financial Officer Tsutomu Nishiyama come to Washington, and it was on the 7th that we were discussing various matters. However, everything went to naught with the attack on Pearl Harbor, but I sincerely feel that we had missed a golden opportunity.

After the negotiation had ended in misfortune, I was concerned about Baruch thinking that I had been a camouflaged envoy and harboring a feeling that he had been betrayed by Kurusu. However, just as we were about to leave aboard the exchange ship, I was told by Desvernine through Akira Miyazaki, manager of the New York branch of Mitsui bureau, that Baruch wanted me to feel at ease since he fully understood my feelings.

The power of the trend of times is indeed strong. Lately, the phrase "Japanese-American economic cooperation" is being used in newspapers and magazines as a matter of fact word. I am looking at this with deep emotions. Whenever I hear of Japanese-American cooperation, I recall with a feeling of gratitude the face of that gentleman, Baruch.

Now, I would like to present the complete text of the original letter I sent to Baruch after the war.

Karuizawa, July 7th, 1947
Mr. Barnard M. Baruch
New York City
U.S.A.

Dear sir;

Ever since the war ended, I have been anxiously waiting for some good opportunity of writing to you. Now this excellent chance having been offered by General [Charles A.] Willoughby's kindness, I first hasten to thank you very deeply for the most valuable assistance you gave me in Washington at the last stage of the unfortunate negotiation. My mission failed and very few people know about what you tried to do to help me.

But some day when the whole story of that negotiation will be made known to the public, the appreciation of our people for your endeavor will surely be profound and everlasting.

Perhaps, you noticed that soon after Japan's surrender, the press reported that there were some prominent Americans outside of the U.S. government who were assisting Ambassador Nomura and myself. I was asked by an Associated Press correspondent who those Americans were. But I declined to reveal those names telling him that I am not in a position to do so, until those gentlemen themselves indicate their willingness to have their identities known. It is how the matter still stands so far as I am concerned.

Secondly I wish to tell you that on the eve of my departure from New York, in June 1942, on board the "Exchange Ship," I duly received Mr. Desvernine's message which was verbally transmitted to me by Mr. Nishiyama of Mitsui Co. I was made to understand that you and Mr. Desvernine were finally convinced that I was collaborating with you with the utmost sincerity. You will certainly appreciate how happy I was to get that message at that moment, when the popular resentment against me was running very high in America.

I presume that there are many Americans who are still persistent in their belief that I had been dealing with the American side with a treacherous intention of giving a false sense of security, in order that the Pearl Harbor attack might be successfully carried out. Quite naturally, I have been very anxious to deny such mistaken charges. As a matter of fact, at several press interviews after the war, I tried to refute such accusation most emphatically. But I was very disappointed to find out that the public prejudice is still too strong and any denial on my part can do very little to rectify wrong impression.

However, now the International Military Tribunal for the Far East is functioning in Tokyo. Many eminent judges and lawyers from various allied nations have been working for more than one year for the investigation of war crimes. They have all important evidences on their hands, and every witness they desire is ready to respond to their call. All telegrams exchanged between us and Tokyo are in their possession, completely deciphered and translated and I have already been questioned several times by the judges of the prosecution section. But so far I have not been indicted on any charge of war crime. I presume if my name may yet be left out of the list of the accused at the end of the trial, even those who have been most persistent in their suspicion will then be convinced that I was not guilty.

Confidently waiting for such a day, I am now quietly living in retirement in this mountain resort. It is a rather trying affair and calls for a great deal of patience and sacrifice on my part and that of my family. But after all it is the price I naturally have to pay for the risk I volunteered to take, in my eleventh hour effort to save the situation for my country. Under such circumstances, I beg to assure you, that it has always been a source of great encouragement to think that a man of your wide and varied experience in state affairs believed in my integrity all through our collaboration.

It was all wrong for Japan to go to war. I knew it and did all I could to prevent it. But after the war once started, I felt it my duty to stand up for Japan and defend her cause as best I could. After all Japan is my country and I love her. If they are going to punish me for what I have written or spoken during the war, either by the legal indictment or the "purge," I will accept it and wait for some future historians to give me their final verdict.

Since the end of the war, many important facts which had hitherto been kept secret have been revealed about that negotiation in Washington. For instance, it has now become known that your Secretary of State had once prepared a compromise plan of three months "modus vivendi," but almost at the last moment the plan was abandoned and that fateful note of November 26th was handed to us in its place.

On our side, I was told, upon my return to Tokyo in August 1942, by General Tōjō himself, that if the personal message of President Roosevelt to our Emperor had arrived just a few days earlier and that American note of November 26th had been somewhat more conciliatory, it would have been impossible for Japan to go to war. Yet it was on that very 26th of November almost ten days before the President's message was actually dispatched, that Ambassador Nomura and I had proposed to our government an exchange of personal messages between the two heads of state. That proposition of ours was chiefly based upon the suggestion made by the Rev. Stanley Jones and some other Americans at that time. However, I now found out that this proposition had never been brought to the attention of either His Majesty or the Prime Minister.

I know perfectly that it is of no use to recount such matters after everything was lost. As our old proverb says, "it is useless to keep on counting the age of your dead child." But in the midst of our present pitiful economic conditions, I cannot help "weeping over the spilt milk." Suppose your Secretary of State had handed over to us his original plan of compromise instead of his final note, suppose again that our suggestion for an exchange of messages between the two chiefs of state should have been accepted by our government, suppose finally that your plan of a solution should have been given a chance to be worked out by our government, the history of the world would certainly be turning an entirely different course now. By precipitating the Pearl Harbor attack, Japan chose war for peace, destruction for construction, economic ruination for prosperity. The Japanese people should someday be told what a golden opportunity they lost.

You must already have heard so much about the remarkable success of General MacArthur's occupation policy, and also about the deep gratitude which our people feel toward this great soldier statesman and the army under his supreme command. It will be quite superfluous to repeat and reiterate it here. But in spite of it all, what the future holds for us is far from being bright. Of course, the economic chaos is a worldwide phenomenon. Even some of the victorious nations are not free from it. From some point of view, perhaps, Japan is faring far better than she deserves. But there is something fundamental in our economic predicaments. They are not only those of a transitory nature common to all nations after a great war, and such call for special measures of solution.

Our inflation, for instance, is a phenomenon caused by purely economic reasons, as it is in elsewhere, but there must also be a unique psychological side to it. Any measure which will serve to restore our confidence as a defeated nation must be very useful in arresting the present inflationary tendency. Therefore, if all leading banks in Japan get together and organize a syndicate and succeed in soliciting the participation of some powerful American banks which are now preparing to operate in this part of the world, it will certainly go a long way toward the reestablishment of the public confidence. And if this syndicate thus organized announces to accept long term deposits in Yen which through some necessary arrangement with our government, may enjoy a certain priority in being converted into U.S. dollars in future by depositor's choice a considerable amount of our currency which is now hoarded by the people will rapidly be accumulated into the hands of this new international organization. Besides, the syndicate will serve as an excellent intermediary for American trade and investment here later on. Such a cooperative plan is an ordinary business transaction among banks and does not necessarily involve any special loan or credit arrangement which they talk about now. But the effect of such cooperation will be very far reaching in regaining a popular sense of security and in checking our present inflationary trend.

Of course, it is only one of the manifold measures which we have to take in surmounting the difficulties which confront us now. Besides, such a scheme might even prove to be a pipe dream of a layman in economic matters. What I most earnestly pray for at this juncture is that some practical suggestion along this line may be forthcoming from a personage of international renown like your good self, and may render its powerful contribution in restoring public confidence here and elsewhere.

Assuring you of my pleasure in being able to have this opportunity of communicating with you and thanking you again for your friendship and assistance at Washington I remain

Very sincerely yours,
Saburo Kurusu

Now remains the memo of Finance Officer Nishiyama, which recalls that period.

Nov. 28 Friday D. K. N. (meaning meeting of Desvernine, Kurusu, and Nishiyama),
Nov. 29
Nov. 30 B. D. K. (meaning meeting of Baruch, Desvernine, and Kurusu)
1 (Mon)
2 (Tues)
3 (Wed) B. Roosevelt (meaning meeting of Baruch and President Roosevelt)
4. (Thurs) B. Nishiyama (meaning meeting of Baruch and Nishiyama)
5.
6.
7. War
10. Tentative schedule of 2nd meeting between Baruch and President Roosevelt.

Chapter 18

The Final Ultimatum

On 30 November when the time limit was about to end, I received an international telephone call from Chief Kumaichi Yamamoto of the American Affairs Bureau. The code used in this conversation was given to me beforehand in the message of the 26th from Tokyo. Since it was an urgently made and very imperfect code, there were many instances of unclarity of meaning during the conversation. In other words, he relayed the very seriousness of the situation in Tokyo and, at the same time, urged me to continue my effort.

Later, the message[1] from our government received on 3 December first refuted the statement made by Secretary of State Hull during meeting of 1 December and then instructed me to explain to America that our counter-plan of 20 November "is believed to be the best means for the breaking of the deadlock at this time." It further stated that they believed our position conflicted in no way with that of America's in as much as our demand for discontinuation of aid to Chiang meant after the negotiation of a Sino-Japanese peace through the introduction of the President. However, on the other hand, war had already been decided upon at the imperial conference of 1 December. In spite of this, they gave us no information in regard to this fateful decision.

On the day before we received this message, Under Secretary of State Sumner Welles who had substituted for Secretary of State Hull, who was ill, requested us to call. He handed us a document, stating that it was the direct order of the President. It pertained to the recent strengthening of our troops in the Southern French Indo-China area. That is, opening with the assumption that since such large force could not be thought necessary for the maintenance of peace and order in said area "it appear to be an indication of the use of troops by Japan for the purpose of further aggression," it stated that such aggression could be surmised as being aimed at the Philippines, the Netherlands East Indies or Malaya, or to be a plan to occupy Thailand by force or armed action, and it requested us to inquire of our government the significance of the recent rapid concentration of troops in French Indo-China since America's attitude regarding aggression against China was well known and had been repeatedly transmitted to Japan. It concluded with the statement that "the reasons why I want to know of Japan's intention are for the above reasons and for the comprehensive problem called America's national defense."

In other words, it was a harsh document of warning announcing beforehand that appropriate actions would be taken in terms of "America's national defense" depending on Japan's reply.

After glancing through this document, we explained to the Under Secretary of State that it was because of our consideration of the development of this type of situation that we had made the proposal of the 20th, that the Japanese people, suffering from America's economic oppression, were being forced into one of the two following predicaments. To yield or to struggle through in some manner and that in view of the present frame of mind of the Japanese people, who, as repeatedly mentioned, have continued the Sino-Japanese incident for four years, we hoped that these points would be taken into consideration.[2] We stated that this document would be forwarded to our government immediately, but we believed America's recent proposal to be absolutely impossible in its entirety as a basis for discussion, that in view of America's plan[3] of 21 June and our plan[4] of 25 September formulated with such painstaking effort by both parties, it was very regrettable that they should be completely set aside and a new plan proposed. Since Japan, to begin with, had stated that she would withdraw her troops from French Indo-China should the Sino-Japanese incidents be settled or a just peace in East Asia be established, the problems mentioned in this document would be resolved naturally once we disposed of basic problems.

In reply, the Under Secretary of State explained that the new proposal of the 26th had been made out of the necessity of clarifying America's basic policy in view of her domestic situation, and he promised to replay our opinion to the Secretary of State.

Then, as we were about to leave, the Under Secretary of State addressed me, in particular, stating that he had heard of me from mutual friends and that if there was anything he could do, he would be willing to discuss it. He had meant American Ambassador to Brazil Carlos Martins and his wife. This was the first time I had met Under Secretary Welles, but he impressed me as being a very polished diplomat.[5]

The document received from the Under Secretary was immediately wired to our government, but our government's reply[6] was very brusque. It stated that the rumor of the strengthening of our troops was considered to be an exaggerated report of the strengthening of our troops in a section of Northern French Indo-China initiated primarily for the purpose of preparing against the Chinese troops recently active along the border, and of the normal movement of our troops in the southern area in conjunction with this, and that our troop strength remained within the limits of the Japanese-French agreement.

As we saw it, when compared with the reports believed to be in the hands of America then, this response would hardly be satisfactory to them. On the other hand, the President had declared at the press conference immediately upon his return from Warm Springs that an inquiry regarding the question of the strengthening of troops in French Indo-China was presently being made of Japan.[7] As a result, the situation was such that it was unlikely that the newspapers would not pick this fact up and editorialize that here was the key to war or peace between Japan and America.

Consequently, we, who were unaware that the government had held an Imperial conference and had already decided on war, were deeply concerned about the situation and requested[8] the government to give us a reply clarifying our peaceful intentions a little more if it desired a settlement of the negotiation or at least hoped for the continuation of the negotiation. However, our government's reply[9] was that it was impossible to explain any further since it involved a secret.

Therefore, Ambassador Nomura and I called on Secretary of State Hull on 5 December. We handed to him the reply of our government pertaining to the question of the strengthening of our troops in French Indo-China in a written form, and Ambassador Nomura primarily undertook the task of explaining the question regarding the strengthening of our troops. The details are as stated in Ambassador Nomura's book, but as late as 5 December we on the spot were still pressing, as instructed, for the reconsideration of our 20 November proposal.[10]

The following night, 6 December, an announcement that the President had sent a message to the Emperor was made. At the same time, the Department of State issued a report that there were 125,000 Japanese troops in French Indo-China and two divisions under the escort of warships appeared to have finally become critical.

7 December was Sunday. I heard from Naval Attaché Ichiro Yokoyama, who had called in the morning, that many messages seemed to have been delivered to the Embassy office. I immediately called Councilor

Sadao Iguchi on the telephone and inquired and was told that all had been routed.

Then, I received a report from Secretary Yuuki that the "Imperial government's opinion," mentioned in the government's instructions of 28 November, had arrived.

Since numerous messages had arrived simultaneously that morning, there appeared to have been considerable confusion in the Embassy office and the wireless room. That is, dispatch #901 stating "The memorandum has been sent, but since it is a lengthy one, part of it may come in tomorrow. Keep the receiving of this memorandum a secret. The time for its submission will be wired later," and 14 dispatches comprising the entire memorandum and dispatch # 907 reading "Hand the memorandum directly, if possible, to the Secretary of State at 1 p.m. of the 7th" practically arrived simultaneously from the evening of the 6th to the morning of the 7th.[11]

The final message specifying the time for the handing over of the memorandum arrived at about 10:30 a.m. of the 7th, and since instructions to the effect that typists should not be permitted to type the memorandum for the preservation of its secrecy, a higher grade secretary, who was not adept at typing, began typing it from the morning of the 7th. As he was excited, causing him to make erasures and corrections, it did not progress as quickly as expected. Secretary Yuuki reportedly stood patiently beside him as though pressing for it.

Ambassador Nomura, too, was considerably worried, and as it became evident that the important memorandum would not be ready by 1 p.m., the time arranged with Secretary of State Hull, the appointment was unavoidably put off to 2 p.m. I, together with Ambassador Nomura, went to the State Department. As we were made to wait awhile, it was 2:20 p.m. when we finally met with the Secretary of State.

After looking at the clock in the room and announcing the time to us, the Secretary of State began reading the memorandum[12] which was handed to him. In the meantime, the excitement gradually caused his hand holding the memorandum to begin shaking. Finally after having finished reading it, the Secretary of State made the now historically famous remark, "Throughout the nine months of negotiation, I never did say a lie and in my fifty years of public service, I have never seen a document so full of fabrication and falsehood."[13] After we had heard this, we silently left the Secretary's office.

As this was Sunday and the meeting had been arranged suddenly that morning, there were not many people at the Department of State and practically no reporters when we arrived there. When we were about to leave, they began gathering gradually, but we refrained from replying to their inquiries and returned to the Embassy.

It was then that we heard the news of the attack on Pearl Harbor. As soon as the automobile we were riding entered, the front gate of the Embassy was closed and the police started warding off the crowd which began to gather.[14]

When I entered my room upon returning to the Embassy, I saw Finance Officer Tsutomu Nishiyama standing dumbfounded. As he was an expert on finance and economics and had been residing in and studying in America for many years, he knew better than anyone else that Japan absolutely would be no match for America in protracted war. For this reason, he had been assisting Ambassador Nomura and doing his utmost for the success of the negotiation from its very beginning.

Nishiyama and I were friends of the same school and class and in close relationship. He had been assisting me as though it was his personal responsibility. As I have stated previously, my meeting with Baruch was through his assistance. The reason he happened to be in my room that day was to make arrangements for establishing liaison with the quarters concerned in as much as Baruch's scheme appeared to be very promising and Baruch was very confident and was scheduled to meet with the President again on the 10th. With a feeling that we lacked the one thing needed, we blankly stared at each other and could think of nothing to say.[15]

In the meantime, Military Attaché Saburō Isoda, with tears in his eyes, came to my room and expressed his sympathies. The other members of the Embassy all had a dejected look. I certainly was deeply moved by the varied feeling of sympathy shown by these people toward me, who had failed in an important mission.

Chapter 19

Life during Internment

Simultaneously with the outbreak of war, the Embassy was guarded, inside and out, by members of the Federal Bureau of Investigation of the Department of Justice and the police. Some crowd appeared to have gathered daily outside of the front gate, but they appeared to have come purely out of curiosity.

As my contact with the outside had suddenly been cut off and the goal toward which I had given every fiber of my being had vanished just as suddenly, I had a feeling of absent-minded emptiness. All I could exert myself to do were to read the newspapers, listen to the radio, and indulge in absurd talks; to feel so composed as to think or write was absolutely impossible. My daily routine became that of pacing back and forth with the other members of the Embassy on the balcony-like place readily accessible from the reception room in place of strolling.

In the meantime, all of the members of the Embassy and their families, who had been living outside of the Embassy, came to be interned within the Embassy. As the number of persons living within the Embassy increased suddenly, two or three others besides Nishiyama, brought in folding beds to sleep in my room at night. At meal-time, even the dining room of the Embassy, big as it was, was filled to capacity and became very congested.[1]

Soon after the outbreak of war, Spain was selected as the country to represent Japan's interest in America. Members of the Spanish Embassy, including Ambassador Don Juan F. Cardenas, came to visit us often and kindly attended to our various needs. Among them, Marquis Morina, councilor of the Spanish Embassy, who had become acquainted with my family while serving in Tokyo, did special favors for me, such as to wire my family of my safety and to even send them a Christmas message.

After Christmas, it was decided to move us to Hot Springs, Virginia. As we were being driven in a number of automobiles from the Embassy to the railway station, we saw no demonstration of any kind along the route, nor on our way aboard the train. Even the members of the FBI, who accompanied us as guards, were very considerate and cheerfully talked to us, and among them, there was one who talked of having played golf with Fumitaka Konoye.[2]

Even when we arrived at Hot Springs, there was only a small crowd believed to be residents living near the station, but nothing of the orindary happened. Although the newspapers and radios were incessantly reporting the war news, the attitude of the American public appeared to be very calm.

The hotel called Homestead, in which we were interned, impressed us as being elegant and sedate.[3] Even the attitude of the hotel employees toward us was not the least bit like what would be shown toward enemy nationals, and they practically seemed to ignore the fact that war had begun. Thus, amidst such circumstances, we welcomed New Year's Day of 1942.

At the beginning of our internment, the area assigned to us for strolling was already restricted to within the surrounding of the hotel. Temporary watch-sheds were created at several places on the outer edge of the grounds surrounding the hotel, but there seemed to have been created as a precaution against those who might try to cause us harm rather than to guard against our escape.

This happened after the guard against us had been eased, the area for strolling had been widened considerably, and the guards had been removed from the watch-shed. According to the discovery made by one of the younger men of our group, there reportedly was scribbled on a panel in one of the watch-sheds, "I don't know which one is Kurusu, but I'd like to wring his neck." I wonder if this truly did not indicate a portion of the feeling of the American public toward me at that time.

After our transfer to this place, members of the Japanese consulates of various areas, including New York, and correspondents began arriving gradually. Then, members of cultural centers and of Mitsui, Yokohama Specie Bank, and other Japanese firms, who had been interned at the immigration station on Ellis Island and in the barracks of various localities, were gradually transferred to this place. Whenever those new people arrived, the situation at various places at the time of the outbreak of war and thereafter and the treatment at various campus were recounted, and we listened intently to these reports.[4]

As our member increased greatly in the meantime, various types of committees were organized. Each of these committees were assigned to dispose of matters ranging from negotiations with the State Department representatives and the Department of Justice inspectors, liaison with the representatives of the Spanish Embassy who came to call on us often, and various negotiations with the hotel to problems of educational training for children, adult educational programs such as lectures and language instructions, and recreation.

As the weather became gradually warmer in the meantime and the area for strolling had been gradually widened, the younger men became very active in sports, finally leading to the formation of teams among themselves and the playing of baseball games against each other.[5] In regard to the limits of the strolling area, a rope was merely strung to indicate it and there were no guards. Within the grounds of the hotel, other sports such as swimming and Ping-Pong were actively planned, and we were even permitted to buy freely at the store within the hotel. At night, we were able to see movies at the theater within the hotel. Other than for medical treatment, strolling beyond the limits of the strolling area was not permitted, and when I obtained permission to visit the dentist, for example, FBI agents accompanied me on each occasion and kept constantly close to me, even to the extent of entering the dental office.

Among the employees of the hotel, the most humorous individual was the proprietor of the barber shop. In as much as he reportedly was formerly a barber for a side-show at Palisades Park, an amusement center in New Jersey, he was a voluble talker, commenting on political economies and relating his experiences of operating a farm, then suddenly talking on the internal situation of labor unions. Since he even discussed his philosophy concerning modern women, I often found it very enjoyable to sit in the chair of the barber shop and listen to his personal views.

Later, we were transferred to White Sulphur Springs, West Virginia.[6] Our hotel was the famous Greenbrier, where Secretary of State Hull reportedly came to rest and even the late Ambassador Hiroshi Saito had often stayed. At Hot Springs, only we Japanese were interned, but the German diplomats of North, Central, and South America and their families were interned here at this hotel before us.[7] Naturally, invitations to tea parties and cocktail parties came to be exchanged between the Japanese and Germans, but the American authorities placed no restrictions against such activities.

The American treatment during our internment was wholly based on the principle of reciprocity.[8] For example, if the radios of the members of the American Embassy in Japan were confiscated, they would take up ours. The buying of literature, which was unrestricted at Hot Springs, was later changed to buying from a specified list after obtaining permission.

Even the limiting of our newspaper to the *New York Times* appeared to have been based on this principle of reciprocity.

Even after we were transferred to this place, the younger men were very active in sports, but because of lack of space, tennis, instead of baseball, became their main interest. Even the school for the children became well organized, and with Tamon Maeda as Principal and a ratio of one instructor for every two students, a very extravagant elementary school with instructors having college degrees came into existence. The enrollment of adults, too, in various language classes increased greatly and even the lectures became very interesting, resulting eventually in one of the secretaries of the Embassy giving an English lecture on Japanese constitutional history upon the request of the German diplomats. There were even some who were seen teaching the German to play Japanese checkers in the hotel lobby.

Chapter 20

Several Speculations

As I did not take part in sports too much and was practically unskillful in games, I spent my six months of internment only in reading and thinking, outside of the daily walks in the yard and swimming in the pool occasionally.

The questions which occupied my mind were, of course, pertaining to the Japanese-American negotiation. These were considering it from the general trend of history—was this negotiation destined to rupture, with what frame of mind did America enter into the negotiation, was it really good from the standpoint of the whole situation that I participated in the negotiation, and in as much as the negotiation had failed, how can the war be brought to an end? Even when reading a book or a newspaper, my attention was always automatically drawn toward these questions.

What I mean is that these speculations only started from this time and not a few of them still recur in my mind, while still remaining unsolved today.

The first question concerning the fatal trend of the Japanese-American negotiations is probably a question of world history to be left for the future. If this field of vision for its study were to be considered from the standpoint of world history, I wonder if a real conclusion cannot be reached by going far back into the history of Eastern and Western culture coming into contact with each other and widely taking into consideration the trail of the advent of western influence into the Orient, instead of restricting it to only the very recent Japanese-American relations, and then placing the basis for its study on it to obtain the under-current of the immovable situation.[1]

From this point of view, I read, as though for the first time, H.G. Well's *History of the World*, which I purchased from the book-store in the hotel, during my internment. I also read Prof. A. Whitney Griswold's *The Far Eastern Policy of the United States* and Prof. Samuel Flagg Bemis's *A Diplomatic History of the United States*, both of which I had subscribed through the book store. The details of the possession of the Philippines by America and the accounts of the marked interest temporarily manifested by America toward Manchuria after the Russo-Japan War, that is, the activities of American Consul-General Willard Straight in Manchuria and Secretary of State Philander Knox's proposal of neutralization of the Manchuria railway, as explained by those two American diplomatic historians, in particular, stirred up my attention anew, and it is needless to state that the situation before and after the Washington Conference, which, regardless of what may be said, became the basic point of conversion of the Japanese-American relations, and the circumstances leading to the abrogation of the Anglo-Japanese Alliance became anew the subject of my speculations. However, we must wait until after the residual fever of this war has completely cooled for an impartial study and comment by the historians of the world concerning the historical connection and causality between these historical facts and the recent Japanese-American negotiation.

The next is the question of the frame of mind with which America entered into the negotiation with me. In studying this proposal, the important thing is the American proposal[2] of 16 April 1941. Considering it from later developments, it could be considered to have been the most favorable opportunity for the successful conclusion of the Japanese-American negotiation, and in spite of the fact that it was very favorable to our country, she refused to accept it. Later, the situation continued to become aggravated and the favorable opportunity for the readjustment of the Japanese-American relations disappeared. It must be considered from this important fact.[3]

The reason I had embraced high hope for the future of the Japanese-American negotiation when, as mentioned previously, I stopped over in Washington on my way back from Germany and even touched upon it in my audience with the Emperor was that there existed in Washington an atmosphere, which, after all, gave me a premonition that some sort of beneficial proposal would be made to us by America then. The reason Prince Konoye, in a discussion of this problem immediately afterwards, deplored the fact that favorable opportunities were always being passed up because the understanding of each of the numerous circles must be obtained in disposing of important diplomatic proposals in Japan was that there probably were indications that Japan would have to let the opportunity slip by in spite of the fact that the most favorable opportunity for a Japanese-American compromise would be presented by this proposal, and I presume the Prince had complained of this situation.

At any rate, on considering it now, it was a conciliatory American plan that makes us wonder what made America concede to such an extent.

The fact that our country did not accept it then is a point that should not be forgotten by those studying the subsequent developments of the Japanese-American negotiation.

This important proposal of America is published in its entirety in Prince Konoye's *Effort toward Peace* (page 39 and 43), published after the war, while the English version is published in the beginning of the appendix in Ambassador Nomura's book. Since the number of persons who, as far as I know, have read it is believed to be less than expected, I am taking the trouble to repeat it and cite only its important points.

In its preamble, it states that Japan and America "accept the mutual responsibility to negotiate and conclude a general agreement" for the restoration of their traditional friendship and resolutely flings aside the adherence to past circumstance, which tended to hamper the conciliation between the two countries in the past, as "in regard to the causes leading to the recent estrangement of relations between the two countries, they, particularly, shall not be discussed." Furthermore, hoping for a speedy conciliation, it regarded protracted negotiation as "inappropriate" and "irresolute" and showing America's unusual eagerness for a speedy conciliation, it proposed that "the understanding be restricted to important pressing problems."

Even in regard to the aims of the agreement, it stated in its preamble that "it is the sincere wish of both governments to establish a peace based on morality in the Pacific, to eliminate the threat of the deplorable confusion, which is about to destroy civilization, and to immediately prevent it from expanding," if impossible, "indicating a determination embracing a very important understanding to the preventing of the European war from spreading into the Pacific."

Furthermore, as the contents of the agreement, it lists the following items:

1. The international and national ideologies embraced by Japan and America.
2. Attitude of both governments toward the European war.
3. Relations of both governments to the China incident.
4. Naval and air strength and maritime relations in the Pacific.
5. Trade and financial cooperation between the two countries.
6. Economic activities of both countries in the Southwest Pacific area.
7. Policies of both governments concerning the political stability of the Pacific.

Concerning these items, it hoped for the readjustment of the relations between the two countries through the "Clarification and improvement of the situation."

Now, the gist of the agreement proposed in connection with each item was as follows;

1. International and national ideologies of both countries.

   Explaining that "each country and each race shall form a Universal Concordia by cooperating with each other," it already specified a clause of particular importance to our country to the effect that both countries "possess the firm determination to prevent the domination of foreign ideologies running counter to these" upon recognizing the so-called idea of Universal Concordia and promising to preserve the national and social ideologies and moral principles based on the tradition peculiar to each.

2. Attitude toward the European war.

   In regard to the Japan-German-Italian Alliance, it specified that in return for Japan's "declaration that its obligation will be invoked only in instances where Germany, a signatory power of the said alliance, is positively attacked by a nation not involved in the European war at present" America will promise to issue a statement that "her attitude toward the European war will not be influenced today or tomorrow by any offensive alliance designed to support one nation and attack the other."

3. Relations of Japan and America to the China incident.

   In regard to the problem of withdrawal of troops, it proposed in paragraph (B) "the withdrawal of troops," from Chinese territories based on the agreement to be concluded between Japan and China" without any specification of time limit and besides suggesting in paragraph (B) that "provided its interpretation and application be discussed between Japan and America at an appropriate time in the future" in regard to the open door policy, it stipulated in paragraph (F) the "merger of Chiang's and Wang Ching-Wei's" regime." Finally in paragraph (H), it proposed "the recognition of Manchukuo." Which has been the greatest obstacle to the Japanese-American relations for the past ten years.

4. Naval and air strength and maritime relations in the Pacific

   It proposed (A) non-intimidation of each other, (B) exchange of courtesy visits between Japan and America fleets and (C) the sailing of some Japanese vessels in the Pacific, based on agreement to be concluded following the settlement of the Sino-Japanese incident.

5. Trade and financial coalition.

   It is stipulated that both countries "guarantee the securing of necessary war materials from the other whenever possessed by the other" and promised to Japan "the restoration of the normal trade relations that existed during the validity of the Japanese-American Treaty of Trade and Commerce." Furthermore, it suggested the supplying of "monetary credit sufficient to realize the Japanese-American economic coalition and the commercial and industrial development for the improvement of the economic situation in the Asia."

6. Japanese-American economic activities in the Southern Pacific.

   It promised America's cooperation and support "in regard to the production and acquisition of such raw materials as oil, rubber, tin and nickel of said area desired by Japan."

7. Policies for political stability of the Pacific.

   It proposed the establishment of the so-called East Asia Monroe Doctrine to the effect that (A) "the acquisition of territories and the annexation of existing nations in East Asia and the Southwest Pacific by European nations in the future shall not be recognized" and promised (B) joint Japanese-American guarantee of independence to the Philippines and (C) amicable consideration toward Japanese migration to America and the Southwest Pacific and their non-discriminatory treatment with the other races.

When those points are considered now, it can be seen that besides the recognition of "Manchukuo" and "Universal Concordia," the various problems, which were the difficult points in the recent Japanese-American negotiation, as well as the various matters which had been the cause of conflict between Japan and America in the past, were practically all to be settled favorably to Japan, and that there was to be laid the foundation of Japanese-American cooperation following the termination of the European war.

This plan, to begin with, was a private plan drafted by "Japanese and American friends of the Japanese," both since Secretary of State Hull, according to Ambassador Nomura's book, told the Ambassador on 16 April to obtain the Japanese government's instructions that it would be alright to conduct the negotiation according to this plan as "it will make America's position difficult, if this should be turned down by Tokyo after the negotiation has progressed," it actually can be regarded as America's formal proposal.

The majority of Japanese, who read this plan today, will wonder why our government did not immediately accept such a favorable proposal. Not only did our government of that period refuse to accept this plan, but the 3rd Konoye Cabinet, which followed, advanced troops into Southern French Indo-China and went far beyond the cutting of Chungking's supply route via French Indo-China, which was the primary aim of the occupation of French Indo-China. Since we, from the standpoint of Britain and America, had assumed a position that would further increase the threat against Singapore and the Philippines, it cannot be said that it was altogether reasonable for America to have felt, as stated to us by President Roosevelt, her first chill.[4]

It was after such developments that I entered the negotiation. As far as time was concerned, it was already past the beginning of the negotiation. Be that as it may, from the impression obtained from the President and the Secretary of State, I believe it would be too hasty to conclude that there absolutely was no intention on the part of America to conclude the negotiation. It appears to be a fact that there were various opinions, both pro and con, in America during the week after the submission of our Plan (B), and according to the diary of Secretary of War Stimson, which I mentioned previously, it appears that Secretary of State Hull was considering a certain type of conditional agreement then, but finally abandoned it for some reason.

What can be particularly considered together with this fact is an article of the *New York Times* of a certain date, which I read during my internment. According to the reports of Arthur Krock, head of the Washington Bureau of said paper, Secretary of State Hull reportedly had, a policy, a desire, to further prolog the negotiation. It could be thought that America, is all probability, expected a change in Japan's attitude through the success of Soviet Russia's counter-offensive along the German-Soviet war front during the period of prolongation of the negotiation and from a military point of view, America was in a position which would become favorable from the standpoint of balance of power the longer she waited.

It can alone be thought that she planned to prolong the negotiation for a while not only from her desire for preservation of peace, but from a practical consideration of these points. At any rate, the attitude of the Secretary of State at the time he handed the note of 26 November did not appear to be too enthusiastic, no matter how it is considered.[5]

Chapter 21

Contemplation and Observation

In regard to the advisability of my having agreed to take part in the negotiation, various thoughts have come to my mind ever since my internment. For example, the Japanese-American war, to begin with, was a war that could not have been started without the consent of the navy. If, by chance, I had not taken part in the negotiation, the navy would have had to take over the entire responsibility for the rupture of the diplomatic negotiation to the deciding of the war in as much as Ambassador Nomura, a senior officer in the navy, was in charge of the negotiation. Then, even the war advocates within the navy might not have been able to decide on war so hastily. Besides, as I had spent almost 25 years of my 35 years of diplomatic life abroad, I had very few friends within the administration. In particular, I was practically an unknown to the army and navy men who were actually running the government of Japan then. Thus, the internal situation was one in which I had practically no power to appeal to those various influences holding forth behind the negotiation, and when it is considered that I, externally, had the handicap of being a signatory of the Tripartite Alliance, the advisability of my participation in the negotiation actually becomes doubtful.

According to a political article written by Mrs. Anne McCormick, which also appeared in the *New York Times* in April of the year following the outbreak of war; Soviet Ambassador Maxim Litvinov, who was stationed in Washington, reportedly stated to several individuals that as soon as he heard that Kurusu was ordered to Washington, he was certain that Japan had decided on war against America. Since this Soviet Ambassador is a total stranger to me, I wonder if he might not have meant that I was powerless against the army and the navy.

It was the same regarding the simple problem of technique of negotiating, which is apart from the so-called basic problems. During the first meeting with the President, he suggested a general Pacific area agreement and even volunteered to be the "introducer" in connection with the Sino-Japanese problem. Why didn't I then immediately and firmly grasp hold of this proposal and work toward obtaining an opening for the settlement of the Sino-Japanese incident, which, to begin with, was the crux of the Japanese-American struggles. Particularly, the attitude of the Secretary of State that day was rather positive, and he had suggested that we return to the State Department immediately after the conferences with the President and continue the negotiation. Besides, I know from the personal instructions received from Premier Tōjō before my departure that he was not placing as great an importance on the question of the Tripartite Alliance, which was stressed during the meeting of that day, as he did on the question of withdrawal of troops.

Indeed, our government, particularly the foreign office, then had a tendency, as mentioned previously, to stress such routine matters as the precise formula of the compromise and the date of signing rather than the crux of such important matters as the cross-road of war or peace. Consequently, it is very doubtful as to whether I could have obtained the consent of our government had I proposed a plan of settlement wholly different from that of our government's instructions at the final stage, and it is also very questionable as to whether I could have even reached the stage of signing the new plan within the short period stipulated by the time limit. At any rate, I am still regretting my lack of resourcefulness in not having been able to strike "while the iron is hot" at that critical time.

Even in regard to the plan to exchange messages between the Emperor and the President, the question as to why I personally did not assume the entire responsibility and make the other party promptly execute it without my having to sound out the intention of our government first is one that I should reconsider.

Among the newspaper articles I had read during my internment, there were not a few that attracted my attention. Of these, the Roberts Committee Report on the Pearl Harbor attack, published in the newspapers of America on 25 April 1942 can be counted as one of the most notable.[1] At that time, I underlined every important point in this report and carefully read them. When I read them, their frankness surprised me. Among them were paragraph 3 of the beginning, which stated, "as the policy of the United States of America in the Pacific clashed with the policies of several other government, the Navy and the War Department of the United States realized that war in the Pacific was inevitable so long as these conflicting policies were not harmonized," paragraph 7, which stated that Japan, in the event of war, first would undertake a surprise attack on the fleet in Pearl Harbor and this attack would come at dawn, paragraph 8 which read that it was expected that Japan would undertake the surprise attack without a declaration of war, and paragraph 9 which reported that the leaders of the Army and the Navy had warned the respective commanders in Hawaii on 27 November that negotiation with Japan had ended in a state wherein the hope of reopening it was absolutely nil.

In as much as war had begun, our greatest concern, of course, was its future development and how, in the meantime, an opportunity for peace could be discovered. From this point of view, I read with interest the newspaper articles pertaining to the war spirit of the American people and America's internal situation. As stated in my report submitted upon my return to Japan, my conclusion was, in general, as follows:

"America has been depending from the beginning solely upon her tremendous economic strength as her greatest power and believes that through its mobilization she can easily make us surrender in the end. On the other hand, the American people, it seems, have come to taste economically some atmosphere of the war only recently through increase in taxes, rise in prices, and lack of some commodities. When considered from a military point of view, the Americans excluding the comparatively few who have relatives at the front, do not feel the war encroaching upon them since not much time has passed since the outbreak of war and many of the battlefields are in faraway places, the names of which they probably did not know before the war. Consequently, they, in general, appear very calm or, when considered from another aspect, very composed in spite of the active propaganda to increase their war consciousness and incite their enmity."

"America, generally speaking, has a geographical position that is practically impregnable against attacks from either Europe or Asia, and many of her mobilization plans, excluding propaganda, are actually progressing smoothly. Even if the situation in the European area should take on an increasingly unfavorable development, there probably will be almost no necessity for America to worry about her own security. Even in regard to her internal political situation centering around coming presidential election, the present government already has been in power for nine years and since it, in the meantime, has established great powers and possesses political power through the various war-time enactments, she has the strength to sway the nation practically according to her will by combining those two factors."

"Even in regard to the opposing Republican party, Wendell Willkie's group which is superior today, has as its platform the encouragement and support of the government and the prosecution of the war, and since AFL and CIO, the two great labor organizations, are both of the same sentiment, we can intelligently estimate that no matter how the war situation in Europe may change, the degree to which it will affect the internal political situation of the present government will be definitely limited so long as no important incident upsetting the balance of political power occurs in the future."

"Since the general situation is such, it cannot be imagined today that America will voluntarily seek peace even if the Soviet-German war should become unfavorable to Great Britain and America in the future."

Now, the 1942 Decoration Day speech of Under-Secretary of State Welles, in which he listed six points and declared America's post-war policy, greatly attracted my attention as an indication of America's intentions concerning the peace terms. On considering America's national situation, which I mentioned previously, together with those intentions of America, I became fully aware of the fact that our work for peace indeed would not be easy.

At the time, the question of India's independence became an active topic of America's public opinion because of Lord Stafford Cripps's mission to India, and the fact that agreements for the liberation of the races in East Asia and for racial equality became active in some quarters in connection with it impressed me deeply. It strongly made me think that we must seriously consider this point in planning for peace in the future.

The joint internment of Japanese and German diplomats at the Greenbrier Hotel continued until May. In the meantime, the German diplomats returned to their country, and it was not until June when we were finally able to return to Japan aboard the exchange ship.

I cannot forget the kindness of the American authorities who were with us from the time at Hot Springs to the time at White Sulphur Springs and particularly Mr. Roy L. Morgan (who is in Japan today as a representative of the Ford Company), who took care of us from the very beginning.[2]

Chapter 22

Exchange Ship

Leaving White Sulphur, we finally boarded the Swedish ship *Gripsholm* at New York at noon of 11 June. However, a troublesome problem occurred at practically the last moment. Because the Japanese government had refused to repatriate certain Americans, the American government, as a counter-measure, refused the embarkation of several Japanese who were scheduled to return home aboard our exchange ship. As a result, the scheduled departure was postponed. The matter, however, was successfully settled through the three-day efforts of Ambassador Don Juan Francisco de Cardenas of Spain, the representative of our interest, and the splendid attitudes of Assistant Secretary Breckinridge Long and others of the State Department.

The exchange ship finally left New York at midnight on 18 June. It was decided that First Class Secretary Lord Silva of the Spanish Embassy would accompany us to Lorenço Marques, Zanzibar [Maputo in present day Mozambique], the exchange point of Japanese and American diplomats. From the Swiss Embassy, which had been selected as the representative of American interests in Japan, it was decided that a Swiss banker residing in New York would accompany us as a temporary member of the legation to meet the American group being returned from Japan.

The committee organized during our internment worked very hard in connection with our embarkation aboard the Exchange ship and took care of the matters ranging from the selection of rooms to the loading of our baggage. In as much as the number of evacuees was large and there were not a few who were pulling up their roots and returning to Japan after having resided in America for many years, the baggage was numerous and mountainous, and the troubles of the committeemen certainly did not appear to be simple.

The concern of not only our committeemen, but those of the captain and his crew were exceedingly great, and since a large number had boarded the ship, which was not too large as a ship for the Atlantic traffic, and since we had not only been delayed a week, but had received no supplies of drinking water or goods to speak of in the meantime while staying off port, it seemed a question as to whether we would have sufficient drinking water for the voyage arose when we finally departed.

With the committeemen as leaders, preparations for the embarkation were made during our stay at White Sulphur Springs. To prepare for an emergency, we received instructions pertaining to boarding life-boats and even practiced first aid for the injured. Furthermore, arrangements were made for look-outs against floating mines and such on a day and night watch system during voyage. When those lookouts took their respective stations after the voyage began, the crew members were rather surprised and appeared to have felt sort of uneasy rather than strange toward our nation until the reasons became clear.

Not long after we had left New York, our ship met an American convoy and the escorts sent up planes, which circled over our ship. Outside of this episode, nothing special that I could recall happened, and we entered Rio de Janeiro on 2 July.

At Rio, Ambassador Ishiuchi and members of the Japanese Embassy in Brazil and a group of Japanese residents were taken aboard. After enjoying the world famous beautiful sceneries of Rio de Janeiro from the deck the entire following day, we sailed from said port on the 4th and continued to enjoy a calm voyage. While enjoying the winter of the Southern Hemisphere where albatrosses flew lazily over our ship with their large out-spread wings, we sailed around the Cape of Good Hope and arrived safely at Lorenço Marques [current day Maputo in Mozambique] on 20 July.

When the ship was finally berthed alongside the quay, German Consul-General Paul Trompke and Italian Consul Umberto Campini came to greet us. Through their kindness, Ambassador Nomura and I were able to go on a sightseeing tour of the city and step on land for the first time in a long while. When we were going ashore then, a foreigner appearing to be a newspaper correspondent, approached Ambassador Nomura and started to say something. As we had been warned by the German and Italian consuls, beforehand, the Ambassador refused to be interviewed and boarded the automobile. However, according to what we heard later, an article purporting to be an interview with Ambassador Nomura at Lorenço Marques reportedly was circulated throughout the world.

On the 22nd, two days later than the *Gripsholm*, the *Asama Maru* and the *Comte Pelde* arrived in port.[1] Amidst a wholly strange circumstance, we saw the Japanese flag for the first time since the outbreak of war and were deeply moved with not a few among us having tears in our eyes. From Japan, Consul-General Takaoka came to greet us. On the 23rd, we were able to board the two ships according to the allocation made through the efforts of the committee beforehand without any great confusion.

The North America group boarded the *Asama Maru* and Southern American group the *Comte Pelde.* The transferring of our baggage, too, was a serious problem and when I saw business executive type men of considerable age carrying the baggage in only their shirts as members of the committee together with the laborers, I was moved with a feeling of profound gratitude.

After the arrival of the *Asama Maru,* Ambassador Nomura and I, who were returning to our ship from the direction of the town, passed Ambassador Grew, who had just come ashore and was heading toward the town, although at a considerable distance. We exchanged greetings by doffing our hats, and a thousand emotions crowded on my mind that instance as I recalled my meeting with him on the eve of my departure from Tokyo.[2]

At Lorenço Marques, the German consul-General, the Italian Consul, and German and Italian residents entertained us with a banquet. When we attended it, we found it to be a very elaborate one and thinking how such a thing could be done in view of the place and a time of shortage of goods, I inquired of one of the sponsors. I was told that the German and Italian residents had all contributed about a week's ration and prepared the feast. Even the musicians and those serving us reportedly were being supplied by the crew members of the German and Italian ships seeking refuge in the harbor at that time. While being moved with a deep feeling of gratitude at the kindness of the German and Italian Consuls as well as the residents, we enjoyed ourselves to our heart's content that night.

At Lorenço Marques, Minister Morito Morishima, who had been newly appointed to serve in Portugal, and several others who were being transferred to the various European areas, disembarked. They were to seek passage aboard a neutral ship and head for their respective place of duty from here, and I can still see in my mind's eye the picture of those people standing on the pier and seeing us off for a long time when our ships finally set sail for our fatherland on the 26th.

We then crossed the Indian Ocean and finally arrived at Singapore. The rubble from the war in Singapore appeared to have been cleared up. Guided by the army and navy authorities, we were taken on a sight-seeing trip of the war sites, the city, and the harbor.

There were many functions held in our honor at Singapore. At a banquet sponsored in our honor by Commander in Chief Hisaichi Terauchi, the chief of staff, who sat next to me.[3] Eagerly described the situation at the time of the outbreak of war, and what caught my ears, in particular, was his explanation of those on the spot confronting difficulty from the standpoint of strategic planning as the opportunity for war gradually slipped by because the military leaders in Japan could not make up their attitude for either war or peace until 26 November. Through this, it became very clear to me that the Japanese government, after all, had decided 26 November as the turning point of our war or peace.[4]

Some of the military personnel and correspondents within our group disembarked from the exchange ship at Singapore and headed for Japan by air ahead of us.

Amidst a storm-like welcome of the crowd, our exchange ship finally arrived at Yokohama on 20 August. Ambassador Nomura and I were immediately placed aboard an automobile, and amidst the ovation of the crowd, we headed straight for the square in front of the palace in Tokyo.

Chapter 23
Arrival Home

Various official functions, such as audience with the Emperor, dinner at the palace, and luncheon with the Prime Minster, followed one after another upon my return to Tokyo. Besides the report made by Ambassador Nomura during our audience with the Emperor, some held the view that I, too, should make a special report, but I believed that since I after all had been sent to assist Ambassador Nomura, it was only proper that the complete details of the negotiation be reported by Ambassador Nomura and that I answer whatever questions asked by the Emperor. It finally was decided in that manner, but when we were received by the Emperor, he asked no question in particular, but only welcomed us with "Thank you for your trouble." I, who had failed in my mission, was filled with trepidation.[1]

At the dinner at the palace, Prince Takamatsu, too, was present.[2] The Prince spoke to me on that occasion and frankly stated that the negotiation had appeared somewhat hopeful for a time after my arrival in Washington and participation in it, but he had been very disappointed when it failed to take a favorable turn after that and finally ended in a failure.[3] On piecing together the remarks made by the Prince then, I came to clearly realize that the Prince had been strongly against war from the beginning.

At the luncheon with the Prime Minister, I was seated next to the Prime Minster. On that occasion, the Prime Minister, turning toward me, regretted the fact that Hull's note was non-conciliatory and, as mentioned previously, he reminisced about the different results if the President's wire to the Emperor had arrived two or three days earlier.

According to what Ichiro Kiyose, former Prime Minister Tōjō's attorney at the Tokyo Trials, that is, the Military Tribunal for the Far East, personally told me when he visited later at Karuizawa, former Prime Minister Tōjō expressed a similar sentiment to Kiyose in regard to President Roosevelt's message to the Emperor, reportedly stating that if the message had come a day or two earlier, the history of the world would have travelled along a different route. This closely agrees with what I heard from the Prime Minister at this luncheon.

Later, while everyone was making themselves comfortable in the reception room after the luncheon, the Prime Minster, together with chief of Staff Hajime Sugiyama, invited me to a corner. I was surprised at their naivetè when they asked me to consider how this war could be terminated quickly, and I remember replying that "working for peace is not as simple as starting a war."

As all of those functions held after my return to Japan came to an end not long afterward, I again requested Foreign Minister Tōgō to accept my resignation, which had been pending since the time of Foreign Minister Matsuoka. He, instead, requested that I assume the directorship and organize a war discussion council with the ambassadors and ministers, who had returned abroad the exchange ship, and after discussing the matter, I recommended Former Ambassador to Brazil Itaro Ishii for the directorship of the war discussion council and decided to remain for a while in the Foreign Office in my previous status. Not long afterwards, Foreign Minister Tōgō resigned because of the problem concerning the creation of the Ministry of the Greater East Asia, and just about this time, I was placed on the waiting list, but received orders to temporarily assume the duties at the Foreign Office.

Later, the foreign minister changed from Masayuki Tani to Mamoru Shigemitsu, but my resignation was continuously held as pending. However, soon after his assumption of office, Foreign Minister Shigemitsu established a Foreign Ministry Advisory Council of three and with Kumataro Honda, Hachiro Arita, and Tadao Yamakawa as the three advisors. I was ordered to attend the advisory council as an envoy awaiting orders. The meetings, generally speaking, were held twice a week, and its arrangement was that whenever there was a request from the Foreign Minister concerning as important mater, each advisor was to express his opinion in regard to it.

Besides the three advisors and myself, former Ambassador to Italy Masaaki Hotta attended practically every meeting, while former Finance Minister Toyotaro Yuuki and President Eiji Amou of the Information Bureau came occasionally. However, to the best of my knowledge, no concrete plan was ever discussed and no matter what views were expressed, the practical difficulty of what to do with the armed services was always confronted.

In regard to this, Kumataro Honda always complained that the "armed services are like society anonym," while Hachiro Arita compared the difficulty of persuading the armed services to catching "one thousand monkeys." Those two advisors were individuals who had plenty of experience in negotiating with the armed services, and I believe it is needless to explain that society anonym meant that responsibility in the armed services was not clear and what the latter meant was that it was absolutely impossible to persuade the whole for there will be one group opposing even if the other group has been persuaded.

Under such circumstances, it was difficult to put into practice the delicate war-time diplomacy. If people were to be mentioned, it invariably would leak out and we would be obstructed or molested, and diplomats were even obstructed by the military police from contacting representatives of neutral countries. In fact, even when I had lunch with a minister of a neutral country, who had sought refuge in Karuizawa, the Japanese servants of said minister were invariably questioned by the military police later. Consequently, the representatives of neutral countries naturally came to avoid contacts with us. Such being the case, it was practically impossible to send out feelers, even if we had a peace plan.

Our country, to begin with, lies geographically in the Far East, and since the diplomatic concept of the nation, historically affected by the 300 years of isolation, was very low and was apt to be dominated readily by conceptual sentimental views, either resolute or weak-kneed, it was always necessary to give special consideration, as compared to the Western and European nations, in carrying out foreign policies. Consequently, such elder statesmen as Munemitsu Mutsu and Jutaro Komura as well as other statesmen in general, practically racked their brains to maintain contact with the internal affairs.[4] Takashi Hara and Tomasaburo Kato, both of whom possessed diplomatic experiences, succeeded in tying together the nation and foreign policy by becoming heads of their party. Generally speaking, the internal affairs and foreign policies began gradually drifting apart following the Washington Conference.[5] In the meantime, many of the people came to be swayed by the militarists' resolute views on foreign policies, which were simple and readily understandable, and finally, there appeared a group within the foreign affairs personnel, who formed a clique and catered to the wishes of the armed services.

Although the internal situation was such, plans for peace were being considered not only by the foreign affairs authorities, but also at least by thoughtful people. Although completely out off from all means of conciliation through Great Britain and America's announcement of "unconditional surrender" and feeling hopelessly difficult, they strove to find some means in between. There were, in general, two ideas. One idea was centered around the Chinese Republic, while the other was around Soviet Russia.

The idea centering around China was one carried out as "the Chungking plan" since the Sino-Japanese incident and aimed primarily for a compromise with Chiang's regime, but after the outbreak of the Japanese-American war, it was developed into the great idea called the Greater East Asian doctrine, which sought peace with Chiang's regime and further developed into an idea seeking for peace with Great Britain and America.

I had this idea early, for in my talks conducted at various places after my return to Japan, I advocated for the liberation of the races of East Asia. For example, in the conclusion of my speech given upon my return to Japan on 26 November 1942, I stated, "If we were to embrace the Greater Eastern Asian Co-prosperity spirit with a determination not to let it end in words only, but to live up to it actually and expand it upon its realization. . ."

"To begin with, the basic fact that the Greater East Asia war developed out of the Sino-Japanese incident and that the Greater East Asia Co-Prosperity sphere forms the crux of the readjustment of the Sino-Japanese relations should never be forgotten by us. Assuming that today the keynote of our national policy concerning the Sino-Japanese incident, namely the idea of co-prosperity in East Asia and liberation of East Asia and the ideals of Konoye's three principles, are being gradually realized, and the policy of the central government, which is attempting to embrace these ideas, and the facilities of the representatives on the spot, which cannot help but conform to the realities, are being fully coordinated, the trend of the Chinese people, regardless of what the policy of the Chungking regime may be, will be the cause and effect mutually with the glorious victories of our imperial army. Thus, an unshakable situation will have been arrested, against which even Great Britain and America can do nothing, and even the important basis of the war aims of the American government, which has adopted aid to China as one of the most important objectives of her fight against Japan, probably will have been shaken.

"As a result, such a sentimental view as "Don't sell China down the river," which was actively propagandized by America just before the outbreak of war, will gradually lose its object, and the fighting spirit of the American people against Japan will bound to become disrupted to that extent. That is, no matter from what point it is considered, our China plan must be considered to be the first requisite of our war-time policy. Among those which have accumulated at the spot over the past five years, there may be situations, which, in all probability, cannot be changed overnight, but the development of the China relations, in a way, can be obtained practically through the sole determination of Japan. In this respect, it can be said that it is rather easier than the other plan which necessitates contending with other nations. Today, when Japan is risking her fate, and East Asia is fighting for her destiny, there ought to be prompt decision suitable for the super-emergency.

"Assuming that the improvement of the situation is being hampered because of the question of face of small local interests, I believe we should remedy it immediately and advance, even a step, toward the direction of real Sino-Japanese amity. I repeat. The realization of the method for the disposition of the incident is, properly speaking, the first requisite of our war-time foreign policy and herein probably lies the most important key to the accomplishment of the Greater East Asia war.

"I won't deal further on the question of our China policy, since I understand that there was a very appropriate opinion submitted recently by Ambassador to China Shigemitsu in regard to this plan and that we are gradually turning toward this direction."

Although this opinion, taking into consideration the positions and susceptibility of the militarists reading it, is written somewhat euphemistically in some aspects, it suggests that the attitude of our militarists and people in China must be changed dramatically at this time and that such things as co-prosperity in East Asia and liberation of East Asia should be steadily carried out, instead of only thinking of and propagandizing it.

This idea gradually gained influence upon the return and subsequent action of Ambassador Mamoru Shigemitsu. Later, when Shigemitsu became foreign minister, he convened the Greater East Asia conference in 1943, resulting in the proclamation of joint Greater East Asia Declaration on the 6th of the month.

I attended this Greater East Asia conference merely as an auditor, but I was introduced to Wang Ching-Wei at the assembly hall and was personally told by Wang that he had read my speech and that he had used it as material for his own speech. Of course, I thought that it included a great deal of compliment, but I, at any rate, felt considerably encouraged on knowing that my contention was being understood by the Chinese. However, what further surprised me was that at the reception luncheon for the Chinese delegation, Prime Minister Tōjō, leaving the guest of honor table and coming directly to the table where I was sitting, unexpectedly inquired of me if the trend of the conference was to my satisfaction.

At any rate, Prime Minister Tōjō strongly intended to carry out the joint East Asia Declaration at that time and he even attempted to send men to the actual locality to encourage it, but those at Shanghai and other places, who understood it and wanted to have it realized, were extremely few.[6] Besides, it was hampered by the antagonism, the greed for power and the corruption of the army and the navy. In as much as the offices of suppliers and accounts of the Army and the Navy were compelled to obtain the necessary materials on the spot, they actively engaged primarily in collecting materials from the Chinese and had no time to consider other matters. Hence, the situation on the spot showed no improvement at all. As a result, the joint resolution, realized at great pains, resulted in "yelling wine and selling vinegar," instead of existing in name only but not in reality, and became good material for counter-propaganda.

The second idea centering on Soviet Russia had existed from prior to the peace between Soviet Russia and Germany through Japan's mediation and even appeared as editorials in magazines. With the development of the war against Great Britain and America, it developed into an idea calling for peace with America and Great Britain through Soviet Russia's mediation after a German-Soviet peace. An excerpt from my written opinion of 8 December 1942, which I mentioned previously, of the portion pertaining to the Soviet plan, is as follows:

"Even immediately after the signing of the Japan-Germany-Italian Tripartite Alliance, the so-called Ribbentrop plan, which attempted to align Soviet Russia in the direction of the Tripartite Alliance, came to be strongly discussed. At this time, there were not a few who agreed to the idea even in our country, and there appeared to be some who went further and regarded it as an important condition for the conclusion of the Tripartite Alliance. Consequently, I have heard that those people became greatly disillusioned when Germany declared war against Soviet Russia, and there were even some who advocated the necessity of amending our attitude toward the Tripartite Alliance compliance with this situation. (Note: Personally told to me by Prince Konoye and referring to the opinion of Teiichi Suzuki). Assuming that it became necessary for Japan, from her autonomous position, to attempt to act as mediator between Germany and Soviet Russia, it is needless to state that very serious attention should be given to the time and method. Moreover, what fundamentally will determine the success of this plan in the event it is to be attempted will be the nature of the peace treaty and the indirect and direct pressure our country will be able to exert upon the nations concerned.

"In view of Hitler's confession, as mentioned previously (Note: Admitted to Ambassador Hiroshi Oshima his miscalculation concerning the war with Russia), it probably would be proper for our country, as an ally, to warn Germany that it, from the standpoint of joint Japanese-German operation, should not make a too excessive demand against Soviet Russia at this time."[7]

"Since there are circumstances wherein Germany has made our country deplore as 'complicated and strange,' her unexpected conclusion of the Soviet-German agreement and has caused some quarters in our country to become secretly disappointed, as mentioned previously, by turning completely around and attacking Soviet Russia, there ought to be no hesitancy on the part of our country to boldly advocate what should be advocated against Germany, while fully paying attention to diplomatic warrants of appointment as warrants of appointment and tests as tests."

In other words, the contention is that if we are to intercede for a German-Soviet peace, we should put pressure upon Germany without any hesitation.

Those two plans, mentioned above, namely, the plan seeking for a peace opportunity centering around China and a similar idea centering on Soviet Russia, were carried out in various forms up to the end of the war. During the early phase of the Koiso Cabinet when I, for personal reasons, exchanged views with people who were close to the Prime Minster, I expressed the following opinion. We should concentrate on China to the very end and firstly send such a personage as Prince Konoye to China to attempt a negotiation that has as its basis the complete return of Manchuria, and in the event she still refuses, we should indicate to China that there is no alternative but to request the assistance of Soviet Russia.[8] If this were to be done, it would be difficult for China to refuse flatly since the matter concerning the future of Manchuria, after all, is being considered. If this talk should succeed and the question of attack on Japan by British and American planes based in China should crop up next, a chance for peace with Great Britain and America with China as the intermediary might be found. In other words, America, Great Britain, and Soviet Russia now have a joint front, and the only way for Japan to break this unity would be to "throw a bone of contention" in the form of Manchuria among them.

Later when someone presented this idea in a written form to Prince Konoye, the Prince reportedly stated that he was in agreement with the view, but he believed the Army and Navy absolutely would not agree and warned that since it would be very dangerous to have such a view in writing, it should be destroyed immediately.

As the war situation became increasingly unfavorable to our country, the idea of seeking peace with Great Britain and America through Soviet Russia's mediation came to be discussed frequently. This idea became an issue at a meeting sponsored weekly by the leaders of Domei News Agency then with former Foreign Minister Arita as the central figure to study our war-time foreign policy. At this time, I had explained that since the consistent policy of Soviet Russia in this war appeared to be the regaining of her lost territories, and she already was gradually carrying out this policy in Europe, she probably would firmly recommend unconditional surrender should her assistance for peace be sought by Japan in as much as it can't be thought that she has forgotten the results of the Russo-Japanese war, and this was merely a circumlocutory observation of mine without the knowledge of the existence of the Yalta Pact. Since these discussion and plans for the promotion of peace, after all, were practically impossible to carry out without the consent of the militarists, it was like a mouse trying to place a bell around the neck of cat and the situation turned from bad to worse to worst. We cannot help but have profound guilty consciences for our faint-heartedness in not having been able to carry them out, although we discussed and I drafted various plans.

What I always think of today is that if there had been some elasticity in the American and British demand for unconditional surrender, the situation probably would have shown greater change prior to the Yalta Pact, but this, in other words, is merely a post-mortem diagnosis.

An event that happened just before the termination of the war and which I always remember is that I was invited to a dinner held in the home of Nobuya Uchida in Karuizawa on the night of 24 July 1945 with Prince Konoye as the honored guest. On the way home, when I was about to get off from Prince Konoye's car, in which I had ridden, near my home, the Prince suddenly asked me to accompany him to his residence. Then, for the first time, he revealed to me that he had received an imperial order to go to Soviet Russia and seek Russia's mediation for peace.

At that time, I was retired from government service with exactly 35 years of service, since my resignation, which had long been pending, had been finally accepted on 8 February of that year. Having refused to remain even as a non-regular staff official, I had absolutely no connection with the foreign office. Consequently, I had no idea concerning the recent delicate turns in our foreign policy.

The Prince began briefly explaining that he had received an order from the Emperor to go to Soviet Russia and that he had accepted it, and showing me copies of the communications between the Foreign Ministry and Ambassador Naotake Sato in Moscow, he asked me for my opinion.

As explained previously, I had advocated sending the Prince to China during the period of the Kuniaki Koiso Cabinet (July 1944-April 1945), and as I knew that the Prince had heard of it, I stated that the direction of this mission differed from that which I had wanted the Prince to undertake. As the Prince agreed to this, I continued and frankly stated that if the trip materializes, that in itself would be a success, but I believed it would be very difficult. The Prince expressed a similar opinion and stated that he thought Soviet Russia would come into the war.

The Prince, then, told me the substance of the talk hold between former Foreign Minister Hirota and the Soviet Ambassador. When I opined that such a talk today was like he and I trying to borrow money from the bank with our homes in Nagata-cho as collateral without knowing that the homes had already burned down, the Prince forced a smile and agreed with me.

According to the newspaper report of that time, Foreign Minister Vyacheslav Molotov reportedly was a day late in arriving for the Potsdam conference. I interpreted this delay of the Soviet Foreign Minister as a result of Japan's request for assistance in peace and stated that I believed that the Foreign Minister probably revealed Japan's request at the Potsdam conference. The Prince held the same view, but I regret to say that we had no idea that an agreement already had been reached among America, Great Britain, and Soviet Russia at the Yalta Conference a half a year before. Not long afterward, the Potsdam Declaration was made public and the Prince appeared to have returned to Tokyo hurriedly, and Soviet Russia, just as feared by the Prince, finally came into war.[9]

As I continued to remain in Karuizawa, I had no knowledge in regard to the political affairs and foreign policies just prior to the termination of the war, and on 15 August, together with my family in one room, I heard with profound respect that unforgettable broadcast of the Emperor.

It was in February of that year that our only son, Ryo, who was a captain in the army air force, intercepted a group of American Grumman planes attacking Japan for the first time and was killed in action.

Notes

Introduction

1. Saburo Kurusu, *Hōmatsu no sanjūgonen* (Tokyo, 1948), p. 84.

2. H. R. Baukhage, the last U.S. journalist to interview Kurusu on December 6, 1941, recorded that he "had a close-up of . . . the world's greatest achievement in diplomatic duplicity." *Mt. Adams Sun*, December 21, 1941 http://mas.stparchive.com/Archive/MAS/MAS12261941P02.php.

3. See the classic study by John Dower, *War Without Mercy: Race and Power in the Pacific War* (New York: Pantheon, 1987). See also Gerald Horne, *Race War* (New York: New York University Press, 2005), Mark Gallichio, *The African American Encounter with Japan and China* (Chapel Hill: University of North Carolina Press, 2000), and Christopher Thorne, *The Issue of War* (New York: Oxford University Press, 1985). For the best study of the Japanese-American internment after Pearl Harbor, see Greg Robinson, *By Order of the President: FDR and the Internment of Japanese Americans* (Cambridge: Harvard University Press, 2001).

4. Cordell Hull, *The Memoirs of Cordell Hull*, 2 vols. (New York: Macmillan, 1948), II, pp. 1062-63. Hull also wrote disparagingly about the appearance of the Japanese envoys: "Nomura sometimes giggling, Kurusu often showing his teeth in a grin, while through their minds must have raced again and again the thought that . . . their government . . . would inevitably bring war with the United States." Hull "felt from the start that Kurusu was deceitful." Ibid., II, pp. 1072, 1074. Hull's wife, Frances, confided to a friend just after Pearl Harbor: "Kurusu is the tricky one. He might have known of the impending attack all along. He might have come all the way here just to delay us and give them time." Diary of Courtney Letts de Espil, December 9, 1941, Espil MSS, Library of Congress.

5. Sumner Welles, *The Time for Decision* (New York: Harper, 1944), pp. 294-95. Assistant Secretary of State Breckinridge Long also noted that Kurusu's purpose was "one of delay." Entry of December 18, 1941, in *Diary of Breckinridge Long*, p. 233. In what was subtitled "The Inside Story of the 'Kurusu Peace Mission,'" journalist Arthur Krock received special access to State Department records, as well as interviews with Hull, and concluded, "Kurusu came on what . . . was forecast as a sleeveless errand . . . under cover of his activities here the Pearl Harbor expedition was launched." Krock, "Infamous Prelude to Pearl Harbor," *New York Times*, November 8, 1942.

6. As quoted in Betty Hite to family, December 7, 1941, Small Collections, Franklin D. Roosevelt Presidential Library, Hyde Park, NY (Hereinafter cited as FDRL). In the immediate aftermath of Pearl Harbor, State Department officials worried that the gentlemanly Nomura—not the "deceitful" Kurusu—would commit ritual suicide, thereby inviting retaliation against US diplomats in Japan. See Entry of December

13, 1941, in Fred L. Israel, ed., *Diary of Breckinridge Long*, p. 229. See also Nomura Diary, December 13, 1941, in Donald M. Goldstein and Katherine V. Dillon, eds., *The Pacific War Papers* (Washington, DC: Potomac, 2004), p. 214.

7. *Prelude to War*, 1943. This documentary film was the most widely viewed of Frank Capra's famous Why We Fight series. In a Hollywood feature film, *Wake Island* (1942), Hawaii-born Richard Loo portrays Kurusu as he stopped at the Wake Island marine outpost en route to Washington, DC, aboard the Pacific Clipper in November 1941. Loo/Kurusu unctuously tells marine officers that he brings a "message of peace" from his "divine" emperor to "your esteemed President Roosevelt." With his heavily accented and idiomatic English, usually delivered in a sneering, sarcastic manner, Loo became the archetype of the Japanese Americans loved to hate in such films as *The Purple Heart* (1944), *Back to Bataan* (1944), and *First Yank in Tokyo* (1945). See also O. C., "The Guilty: Saburo Kurusu," *Collier's Weekly* (June 24, 1944), pp. 68-71.

8. Quoted in Masuo Kato, *The Lost War: A Japanese Reporter's Inside Story* (New York: Knopf, 1946), p. 76.

9. *Kurusu Speaks* (Tokyo: Nippon Times Ltd., 1944), p. 20. As late as 1973, *Reader's Digest* refused to publish a tribute to Kurusu's widow (who had just died) because her husband had been a "liar." Neal Henry Lawrence, "The Unforgettable Alice Jay Kurusu," http://www.asjapan.org/web.php/lectures/2000/05.

10. In her authoritative study of Pearl Harbor, Roberta Wohlstetter writes that the Japanese task force "was under orders to return up to 24 hours before D-day if anything favorable developed in the U.S.-Japanese negotiations." Wohlstetter, *Pearl Harbor: Warning and Decision* (Stanford, CA: Stanford University Press, 1962), p. 202.

11. Kurusu quoted in "Kurusu 'Unaware' of Blow at Hawaii," *New York Times*, September 7, 1945. Kurusu's home had been destroyed by B-29s and his only son, an aviator, had died in 1945.

12. Saburo Kurusu, *Hōmatsu no sanjūgonen—Nichi-Bei kōshō hishi* (Tokyo, 1948) and *Nichi-Bei gaikō hiwa* (Tokyo: Sogensha, 1952).

13. Immanuel C. Y. Hsu, "Kurusu's Mission to the United States and the Abortive *Modus Vivendi*," *Journal of Modern History*, 24 (Sept. 1952), pp. 301-07.

14. See Roger B. Jeans, *Terasaki Hidenari, Pearl Harbor, and Occupied Japan: A Bridge to Reality* (New York: Lexington, 2009) and Peter Mauch, *Sailor Diplomat* (Cambridge, MA: Harvard University Press, 2011).

15. Herbert Feis, *The Road to Pearl Harbor: The Coming of the War Between the United States and Japan* (New York: Atheneum, 1967), 299.

16. See Peter Mauch, "Revisiting Nomura's Diplomacy: Ambassador Nomura's Role in the Japanese-American Negotiation, 1941," *Diplomatic History* 28 (June 2004), pp. 365-370.

17. Quoted in Herbert P. Bix, *Emperor Hirohito and the Making of Modern Japan* (New York: HarperCollins, 2000), p. 202.

18. Tōjō correctly surmised that the Roosevelt administration was pursuing a "Europe First" strategy, as indicated by the growing Lend-Lease supplies to both England and the Soviet Union as well as by naval incidents in the North Atlantic.

19. Kurusu, *Homatsu*, 33.

20. See John Toland, *The Rising Sun: The Decline and Fall of the Japanese Empire, 1936-1945* (New York: Random House, 1970), p. 165. "There were some on the Army General Staff who openly said they wished Kurusu's plane would crash." Eri Hotta, *Japan 1941: Countdown to Infamy* (New York: Knopf, 2013), p. 246.

21. Feis, *Road to Pearl Harbor*, 307.

22. Quoted in *Kurusu Speaks*, 22.

23. Hull memorandum, November 17, 1941, *Foreign Relations of the United States: Japan 1931-1941*, 2 vols. (Washington, DC: Government Printing Office, 1943, II, p. 740 (hereinafter cited as *FRUS*).

24. Roosevelt to Hirohito, December 6, 1941, ibid., p. 786.

25. *FRUS: Japan*, II, pp. 753-55.

26. Hull memorandum of conversation, November 17, 1941, *FRUS: Japan 1931-1941*, II, p. 742. The translation of Nomura's and Kurusu's report to Tokyo quotes Roosevelt as saying, "The United States is not trying to intervene or mediate in the problems of Japan and China. I don't know whether there is such a word in the parlance of diplomats or not, but the United States' only intention is to become an 'introducer.'" Washington to Tokyo, November 17, 1941, #1118, in *The "Magic" Background to Pearl Harbor*, in Department of Defense, 8 vols. (Washington, DC: US Government Printing Office, 1978), IV, Appendix, A-73.

27. Quoted in David J. Lu, *From the Marco Polo Bridge to Pearl Harbor* (Washington, DC: Public Affairs, 1961), p. 223. At about this time, Roosevelt outlined a possible modus vivendi for Hull: "1. U.S. to resume economic relations—some oil and rice now—more later. 2. Japan to send no more troops to Indo-China or Manchurian border or any place South—(Dutch, Brit. or Siam). 3. Japan to agree not to invoke tripartite pact even if U.S. goes into the war. 4. U.S. to introduce Japs to Chinese to talk things over but U.S. to take no part in their conversations." Roosevelt to Hull, n.d., *FRUS, 1941: Far East*, IV, p. 626.

28. Ibid., 223; and Kurusu, *Nichi-Bei gaikō hiwa*, p. 134.

29. Draft letter presented to Hull, November 21, 1931, *FRUS: Japan, 1931-1941*, II, pp. 756-57.

30. Washington to Tokyo, November 23, 1941, #1160, *"Magic" Background*, IV, pp. 1-86.

31. Kurusu, *Nichi-Bei gaikō hiwa*, p. 141.

32. Ibid. In fact, Hull secretly suffered from tuberculosis. Irwin Gellman, *Secret Affairs* (Baltimore: Johns Hopkins University Press, 1995).

33. Hull memorandum, November 21, 1941, *FRUS: Japan, 1931-1941*, II, p. 756.

34. Hull, *Memoirs*, II, p. 1071.

35. See Keiichiro Komatsu, *Origins of the Pacific War and the Importance of "Magic"* (London: Routledge, 2009), p. 307.

36. Hull, *Memoirs*, pp. 1069-70. Foreign Minister Tōgō had described Plan B to Nomura as a "*saigoteki jouhoan* [a final-like compromise plan]" that was mistranslated as "an absolutely final proposal." Tōgō did not intend Plan B as an ultimatum. According to Tosh Minohara, Tōgō merely wanted to avoid a situation where Nomura, "out of his personal zeal to secure peace, would disobey instructions and revise the agreement himself." Tosh Minohara, "'No choice but to rise': Tōgō Shigenori and Japan's Decision for War," in Masato Kimura and Tosh Minohara, eds., *Tumultuous Decade: Empire, Society, and Diplomacy in 1930s Japan* (Toronto: University of Toronto Press, 2013), p. 266. See also Mauch, *Sailor Diplomat*, p. 207.

37. Hull memo, November 22, 1941, *Foreign Relations: 1941*, IV, p. 640.

38. Minohara, "Tōgō and Japan's Decision for War," in Kimura and Minohara, eds., *Tumultuous Decade*, p. 269. For evidence that the Japanese were decoding US cables, including the modus vivendi message, see Seishiro Sugihara, *Between Incompetence and Culpability: Assessing the Diplomacy of Japan's Foreign Ministry from Pearl Harbor to Potsdam* (Lanham, MD: University Press of America, 1997), pp. 48-49.

39. Quoted in Utley, *Going to War*, p. 173.

40. Lord Halifax Secret Diary, November 27, 1941, Borthwick Historical Institute, York, England.

41. The remaining two points asserted that existing agreements with third parties should not be interpreted to conflict with the basic purpose of the agreement in establishing and preserving peace in the Pacific and that both Japan and the United States should use their influence with other governments to gain their support and adherence to the agreement.

42. Ballantine memorandum, November 26, 1941, *FRUS: Japan, 1931-1941*, II, pp. 765-66.

43. Minohara, "Tōgō and Japan's Decision for War," in Kimura and Minohara, eds., *Tumultuous Decade*, pp. 259, 268, 271. Tōgō could "never forget the despair which overpowered me. I had fought and worked unflaggingly until that moment; but I could feel no enthusiasm for the fight thereafter. . . . I tried . . . to close my eyes and swallow the Hull note whole, as the alternative to war, but it stuck in my craw." Quoted in Sugihara, *Between Incompetence and Culpability*, p. 48.

44. Washington to Tokyo, Trans-Pacific Telephone, November 27, 1941, *"Magic" Background*, Appendix, A-113-16.

45. The careful judgment of Nomura's recent biographer, Peter Mauch, is worth noting: "Kurusu was sincere in his efforts at peace. That is not to say that he failed to understand that things stood on a knife edge. However, he did not (could not) have known of the Pearl Harbor plan (knowledge thereof was restricted to a select few within the Japanese navy). Like Nomura, Kurusu guessed that Japanese forces would hit SE Asia if the negotiations in Washington failed. Also like Nomura, Kurusu recognized that such a move on Japan's part would result in war with the U.S. Again like Nomura, Kurusu did not rate Japan's chances in war against the U.S. (although, as Kurusu was a diplomat and not a navy officer his thinking on this score was probably a little less sophisticated than was Nomura's). In any case, all these assumptions meant that Kurusu did everything within his power to see diplomacy succeed. That diplomacy failed was certainly not due to duplicity on Kurusu's part." Peter Mauch to editors, September 2010.

46. It was primarily this coded telephone conversation that prompted the International Military Tribunal for the Far East to conclude that Kurusu knew beforehand that war with the United States was "imminent." See *New York Times*, November 11, 1948. Nonetheless, Roberta Wohlstetter affirms that "U.S. intelligence . . . had more evidence of Tokyo's intent than [did] the Japanese ambassadors." Wohlstetter, *Pearl Harbor*, p. 203.

47. Quoted in Frederick Moore, *With Japan's Leaders* (New York: Scribner's, 1942), pp. 282-83.

48. Entry of November 30, 1941, Richard Casey Diary, in Carl Bridge, ed., *A Delicate Mission: The Washington Diaries of R. G. Casey, 1940-42* (Canberra: National Library of Australia, 2008), p. 204.

49. Halifax to Foreign Office, November 30, 1941, #5496, FO 371/27913.

50. Quoted in Jeans, *Terasaki*, p. 119.

51. Nomura to Tokyo, December 1, 1941, *Pearl Harbor Attack*, pt. 12, pp. 213-14.

52. Nomura to Tokyo, December 2, 1941, #1242, *"Magic" Background*, A-124.

53. See F. C. Jones, *Japan's New Order in East Asia: Its Rise and Fall, 1937-45* (New York: 1954), pp. 319-20.

54. Hoover Diary, November 23, 1941, PPS (Pearl Harbor Events), Herbert Hoover MSS, Herbert Hoover Presidential Library, West Branch, Iowa.

55. Baruch quoted in Kurusu, *Nichi-Bei*, p. 189.

56. Bernard M. Baruch, *Baruch: The Public Years: My Own Story* (New York: Holt, Rinehart and Winston, 1960), p. 289. See also Robert Sherwood notes of interview with Baruch, January 27, 1947, Robert E. Sherwood MSS, Houghton Library, Harvard University, Cambridge, MS; Bernard Baruch to John Toland, November 6, 1961, Box 1, John Toland MSS, FDRL; and Saburo Kurusu to Bernard Baruch, July 7, 1947, Box 121, Bernard M. Baruch MSS, Seeley Mudd Library, Princeton University, Princeton, NJ.

57. Hoover Diary, November 30, 1941.

58. Kurusu's Final Report, June 2, 1942, Gaimusho, ed., *Nihon Gaikô Bunsho: Nichi-Bei Kôshô, 1941*, 2 vols. (Gaimusho: Tokyo, 1990), II, p. 384.

59. Hoover Diary, December 1, 1941. In Kurusu's papers in Tokyo there is a handwritten document (in English) entitled "Kurusu Plan" similar to the Hoover-Desvernine proposal, with "U.S. President 'introducing'" the Japanese to the Chinese Nationalist government; "withdrawal of Japanese troops from F[rench] I[ndo] C[hina]"; "establishment of neutral zone" including Burma, Indochina, and the Dutch East Indies; and agreement that the "Tripartite Pact" would not "interfere" with "the above policy." Memorandum, undated, Saburo Kurusu MSS, National Diet Library, Tokyo.

60. Hoover Diary, December 2, 1941.

61. Roosevelt's appointment calendars do *not* list meetings with Desvernine or the Japanese envoys on December 4 and 5, 1941. See "Roosevelt Day-By-Day," December 4-5, 1941, Pare Lorentz files, FDRL.

62. Hoover Diary, December 3-6, 1941. As early as November 19, FDR had told the Japanese envoys that "at a suitable stage . . . this Government might, so to speak, introduce Japan and China to each other and tell them to proceed with the remaining . . . adjustments." Hull memorandum, November 17, 1941, *FRUS: Japan, 1931-1941*, II, p. 742.

63. Quoted in Richard Norton Smith, *Uncommon Man: The Triumph of Herbert Hoover* (New York: Simon & Schuster, 1985), p. 306.

64. Gary Dean Best, *Herbert Hoover: The Postpresidential Years, 1933-1964*, 2 vols. (Stanford: Hoover Institution Press, 1973), I, pp. 200-203; Smith, *Uncommon Man*, pp. 305-306; and Alfred Castle, *Diplomatic Realism* (Honolulu: University of Hawaii Press), 1997), p. 116. For a detailed account that connects Hoover's peace initiative with parallel efforts by Japanese moderates, see Iguchi, *Unfinished Business*, ch. 7. See also Iguchi Takeo, *Demystifying Pearl Harbor* (Tokyo: International House of Japan, 2009), ch. 20.

65. Quoted in Carl Boyd, *Hitler's Japanese Confidant* (Lawrence: University of Kansas Press, 1993), p. 36. For an excellent historiographical summary, see Michael A. Barnhart, "The Origins of the Second World War in Asia and the Pacific," in Michael J. Hogan, ed., *Paths to Power: The Historiography of American Foreign Relations to 1941* (New York: Cambridge University Press, 2000), pp. 268-295.

66. See for example, Antony Best, *Britain, Japan, and Pearl Harbor* (London: Routledge, 1995); Richard Aldrich, *The Key to the South* (London: Oxford University Press, 1993); Aldrich, "Conspiracy or Confusion?: Churchill, Roosevelt, and Pearl Harbor," *Intelligence and National Security* 7 (1993), pp. 335-346; and Robert J. C. Butow, "Pearl Harbor Jitters," *Prologue* 22 (Winter 1991), pp. 383-391. For Australian

minister Richard G. Casey's participation in the eleventh-hour diplomacy, see Bridge, ed., *Delicate Mission*, pp. 202-208.

67. Mauch, "Revisiting," p. 382. After a meeting with Sumner Welles on December 2, 1941, a dispirited Nomura accosted friendly journalist Wilfred Fleisher of the *New York Herald Tribune* and said, "I see you have joined the war party." Quoted in Wilfred Fleisher, *Our Enemy Japan* (Garden City, NY: Doubleday, 1942), p. 160. A recent article dates the "point of no return" to November 30, 1941, when Hirohito approved the final Imperial Conference decision that sanctioned the Pearl Harbor attack. See Noriko Kawamura, "Emperor Hirohito and Japan's Decision to Go to War with the United States Reexamined," *Diplomatic History* 31 (January 2007), p. 78.

68. Washington to Tokyo, December 6, 1941, *PHA*, Part 12, p. 247. This dispatch was not reprinted in the later publication of *The "Magic" Background to Pearl Harbor*.

69. Embassy dispatch #1272 to Tokyo, December 6, 1931, Gaimusho, *Nihon Gaikô Bunsho*, II, pp. 251-252. For a slightly different translation, see Iguchi, *Demystifying Pearl Harbor*, p. 226.

70. Tōgō to Nomura, December 3, 1941, #876, Gaimusho, *Nihon Gaikô Bunsho*, II, p. 230. Saburo Kurusu, *Hōmatsu no sanjūgonen* (Thirty-five Years in the Bubble) (Tokyo: Chuokoron-sha, 1986 edition), p. 126. Kurusu also recalled that Baruch had suggested that the United States give Japan a billion-dollar loan. See Iguchi, *Unfinished Business*, p. 168.

71. We should note that Hoover's Pearl Harbor "diary" should more accurately be described as an aide-memoire or a retroactively created desk calendar in which Hoover inserted relevant documents and commentary. Hence, the "diary" may contain some inaccuracies as to dates and details. See George H. Nash, ed., *Freedom Betrayed: Herbert Hoover's Secret History of World War II and Its Aftermath* (Stanford, CA: Hoover Institution Press, 2011), p. lviii.

72. See Haruo Iguchi, "Herbert C. Hoover Moto Daitoryō to Nichibei Sensō: Shinjuwan Chokuzen no Hoover Nikki no Shinpyōsei" [Behind-the-Scenes Herbert C. Hoover's Involvement in and Account of U.S.-Japan Diplomacy Right Before Japan's Pearl Harbor Attack], *Doshisha Amerika kenkyū* 35 (March 1999), pp. 103-113.

73. In his report to Tokyo following Hull's ten-point note on November 26, Kurusu had urged an exchange of messages between Roosevelt and Hirohito. His appeal was rejected. See James W. Morley, ed., *Japan's Road to the Pacific War: The Final Confrontation* (New York: Columbia University Press, 1994), pp. 326-327.

74. Entry of November 28, 1941, Joseph Davies Diary, Joseph Davies MSS, Library of Congress.

75. Ibid.

76. For Jones, see *FRUS: 1941*, IV, pp. 306-310, 355-457, 459, 501-502, 555-558, 561-562, 631, 702-703. See also Jones's letters to FDR in Box 2, OF197a, FDRL.

77. Quoted in Edward Behr, *Hirohito: Behind the Myth* (New York: Villard Books, 1989), pp. 242-244, and in Roger Jeans, *Hidenari Terasaki, Pearl Harbor, and Occupied Japan* (Lanham, MD.: Lexington, 2009), p. 115. See also Gwen Terasaki, *Bridge to the Sun* (Chapel Hill: University of North Carolina Press, 1957), pp. 64-69.

78. See also the personal account by E. Stanley Jones in *Asia and the Americas* 45 (December 1945), pp. 609-16. Roosevelt's appointments diary does list his meeting with Jones at 12:15 p.m. on December 3, 1941, "Roosevelt Day-by-Day," Pare Lorentz Chronology, FDRL.

79. Quoted in Robert Dallek, *Franklin Roosevelt and American Foreign Policy, 1932-1945* (New York: Oxford University Press, 1979), p. 309. Roosevelt also called

it a message "from a mortal to a deity." Halifax Diary, December 6, 1941. Roosevelt had told Halifax on December 1 of "his idea of sending a communication direct to the Emperor which he said had been the thing that had worked at the time of the *Panay* incident. The communication would be friendly but would make plain that if the present Japanese attitude continued, war would result. He is, however, suspending this for the present." Halifax to Foreign Office, December 1, 1941, #5519, FO371/27913, British Public Record Office, Kew, England.

80. Halifax to Foreign Office, #5603, December 5, 1941, FO371/27914. Halifax continued, "As to the treatment of Kurusu's approach generally, I said no doubt he would be particularly careful not to put a foot wrong with the Chinese after last week's experience, and that therefore it would be wiser to avoid any detailed suggestion at first stage merely combining with message and warning, a hint that if Emperor's reply gave him any reason to think it would be helpful, he might be able to make a suggestion that would assist in the maintenance of peaceful relations. The President agreed."

81. "Welles has just telephoned to say that the President has changed his mind and wishes to suspend decision about conveying assurance to Thailand. . . . He will discuss . . . message to Thailand with me again when he has made up his mind about [message to] the Emperor. . . . This is most annoying." Halifax to Foreign Office, December 6, 1941, #5612, FO 371/27914, ibid.

82. Henry Morgenthau Presidential Diary, December 3, 1941, Morgenthau MSS, FDRL; and Francis Biddle Cabinet Diary, December 5, 1941, Biddle MSS, FDRL. "It seemed to be the [cabinet] consensus that the Japs were a little less warlike than a few days ago." Entry of December 6-7, 1941, Claude Wickard Diary, Wickard MSS, FDRL. Two other Asian scholars, historian Kan'ichi Asakawa of Yale University and archeologist Langdon Warner of Harvard University, were also importuning the White House with drafts of a message to the emperor. See Tohru Takeda, *Kan'ichi Asakawa: A Historian Who Worked for World Peace* (Tokyo: Taiyo, 2007), pp. 58-66; Theodore Bowie, ed., *Langdon Warner Through His Letters* (Bloomington: Indiana University Press, 1966), pp. 157-160; and R. J. C. Butow, *The John Doe Associates: Backdoor Diplomacy for Peace, 1941* (Stanford, CA: Stanford University Press, 1975), p. 443.

83. Kurusu also disparaged the Tripartite Pact, saying that "Germany was trying to make of Japan an Italy in the Pacific," and he "hoped and prayed that they would not be successful." He realized "in the event of a German victory, the Germans would take the Netherlands East Indies for themselves and give nothing to Japan." Mayer memorandum, December 8, 1941, PSF Japan, FDRL. According to the memoirs of Foreign Minister Tōgō, Prime Minister Tōjō judged Roosevelt's appeal to the emperor to be "too little, too late" but thought that it might have caused "another confusion again" on the Japanese side if the message had been received "one day or two days earlier." Quoted in Komatsu, *Importance of "Magic,"* p. 326.

84. Mayer to H. H. Hoehling, June 11, 1962, John Toland MSS, FDRL.

85. Quoted in Butow, *John Doe Associates*, p. 299. For a provocative argument that American officials misinterpreted the phrase "things are automatically going to happen" because of faulty translations, see Komatsu, *Importance of "Magic,"* pp. 312-313.

86. Quoted in Feis, *The Road to Pearl Harbor*, p. 340. As Chinese ambassador Hu Shih recalled, Roosevelt said he expected "foul play" within forty-eight hours and that something "nasty" might occur in Thailand, Malaya, the Dutch Indies, and "possibly" the Philippines. See also A. A. Hoehling, *The Week Before Pearl Harbor* (New York: Norton, 1963), p. 179.

87. Draft message from President Roosevelt to the Emperor of Japan, December 6, 1941, *FRUS, 1941*, VII, pp. 722-23. As to why Roosevelt may have deleted the stand-still proposal, see the careful discussion in Jon Bridgeman, "Saturday, December 7, 1941," in Robert W. Love, Jr., ed., *Pearl Harbor Revisited* (New York: St. Martin's, 1995), pp. 156-57; see also Wohlstetter, *Pearl Harbor*, pp. 266-69.

88. Langer and Gleason note that Roosevelt sent a simultaneous cable to Chiang Kai-shek urging the Chinese not to criticize his last-minute overture to Hirohito, but did so in language that implies that a ninety-day truce, resumption of oil exports, and Japanese withdrawal from southern French Indochina remained in his message to the emperor. Langer and Gleason, *Undeclared War*, pp. 931-32. For the Japanese reaction, see Komatsu, *Importance of "Magic,"* pp. 341-42.

89. Hull testimony, PHA, Part 2, 5374. State Department official Joseph W. Ballantine also testified that "we thought that the chances were slim that it [Roosevelt's message] might accomplish anything, but in view of the desperate situation we did not want to overlook the slightest chance." Quoted in Iguchi, *Demystifying Pearl Harbor*, p. 287.

90. For details on how military authorities in Tokyo delayed Roosevelt's message until it arrived too late, see Iguchi, *Demystifying Pearl Harbor*, pp. 229-36. See also Komatsu, *Origins*, pp. 326-27. For the emperor's reaction, see Bix, *Hirohito and the Making of Modern Japan*, pp. 436-37.

91. For a persuasive argument that the United States stumbled into war by abandoning "containment" in favor of "rollback" vis-à-vis Japan, see Sidney Pash, "Containment, Rollback, and the Onset of the Pacific War," in G. Kurt Piehler and Sidney Pash, eds., *The United States and the Second World War: New Perspectives on Diplomacy, War, and the Home Front* (New York: Fordham University Press, 2010), ch. 2.

92. Hull, *Memoirs*, pp. 1096-97.

93. William R. Castle Jr. to Herbert Hoover, December 5, 1949, Hoover file, William R. Castle Jr. MSS, Hoover Presidential Library. See also Castle to Kichisaburo Nomura, October 31, 1947, enclosed in Nomura to Eleanor Roosevelt, May 29, 1953, Box 1731, Eleanor Roosevelt MSS, FDRL.

94. Quoted in Morley, *Final Confrontation*, p. 327. Kurusu also warned that Germany would not necessarily support Japan under Article 3 of the Tripartite Pact if Tokyo initiated a wider war in such a manner.

95. Kurusu, *Homatsu*, p. 211.

96. "Everything looks like the Jap balloon going up in . . . day or two—cyphers burnt, secret messages . . . . it looks pretty clear now that the U.S., the Dutch, and ourselves shall all be immediately together." Halifax Secret Diary, December 4, 1941.

97. Ibid., November 29, 1941. Halifax added, "I liked the old boy [Hull] very much."

98. Entry of December 1, 1941, in Beatrice Bishop Berle and Travis Beal Jacobs, ed., *Navigating the Rapids, 1918-1971: From the Papers of Adolf A. Berle* (New York: Harcourt Brace Jovanovich, 1973), p. 381.

99. Jonathan G. Utley comments that Hull showed "classic symptoms of what is nowadays called 'burn-out.'" Jonathan G. Utley, *Going to War with Japan, 1937-1941* (Knoxville: University of Tennessee Press, 1985), p. 175. For Hull's tuberculosis, see Gellman, *Secret Affairs*, pp. 31, 42, 266-67.

100. See R. G. Casey to H. V. Evatt, November 29, 1941, Cablegram 1053, http://www.dfat.gov.au/publications/historical/volume-05/historical-document-95-140.html, and entry of December 1, 1941, Jacobs, *Navigating the Rapids*, p. 381.

101. Nomura to Tokyo, November 27, 1941, #1206, *"Magic" Background*, IV, A-112.

102. Entry of December 1-4, 1941, Diary of J. Pierrepont Moffat, Moffat MSS, Houghton Library.

103. Entry of December 6, 1941, Diary of Mrs. Charles Hamlin, Small Collections, FDRL; Rexford Tugwell Diary, December 4, 1941, Tugwell MSS, FDR; Huston Thompson to his Mother, November 12, 1941, Huston Thompson MSS, Library of Congress; Grace Tully, *FDR, My Boss* (New York: Scribner's, 1949), pp. 249-51. For medical evidence that Roosevelt had to undergo blood transfusions in the spring and summer of 1941 and may have been suffering after-effects in November and December, see Steven Lomazow and Eric Fetmann, *FDR's Deadly Secret* (New York: Public Affairs, 2009), ch. 7.

104. Roosevelt quoted in Morgenthau Presidential Diary, December 3, 1941.

105. *Pearl Harbor Hearings*, II, p. 576.

106. *Kurusu Speaks*, p. 78. Also quoted in *New York Times*, November 27, 1942. For a copy of Kurusu's speech online, see http://www.ibiblio.org/pha/policy/1942/421126a.html.

107. Entry of November 27, 1941, Diary of Henry L. Stimson, Stimson MSS, Sterling Library, Yale University, New Haven, CT.

108. Ironically, Kurusu's memorandum of his conversation with Hull on November 22 quotes the secretary of state as saying, "Real politicians try to seek peace until the last minute." Memo #11, Kurusu MSS, National Diet Library, Tokyo.

109. Memorandum of conversation with Hull, December 11, 1941, Arthur Krock MSS, Seeley Mudd Library, Princeton University, Princeton, New Jersey.

110. Hull, *Memoirs*, II, p. 1101.

111. See the retrospective comments by the ranking expert on Japan in the US Embassy in Tokyo: "You say not once but many times that we in Tokyo could give Hull no substantial reason to support our belief that even a shadowy gesture of conciliation would bear fruit. I think you will admit that our Tokyo record on the question of whether or not Japan would capitulate to American economic and other pressure is, to put it moderately, rather better than Washington's. If we, because of our more exact knowledge of the Japanese mind and temperament, were right when Washington was wrong, would it not be rational and reasonable to think that Grew and I had good grounds for believing that something from Washington in the nature of a crumb of good will could have been effectively used by those Japanese who, if you cannot believe they were our friends, were at least desperately anxious to avert war?" Eugene Dooman to Herbert Feis, July 8, 1949, Box 2, Herbert Feis MSS, Library of Congress.

112. David Mayers, *FDR's Ambassadors and the Diplomacy of Crisis* (New York: Cambridge University Press, 2013), p. 250.

113. Quoted in Evan Mawdsley, *December 1941: Twelve Days that Began a World War* (New Have: Yale University Press, 2011), p. 92.

114. Kurusu's Final Report, June 4, 1942, Gaimusho, *Nihon Gaikô Bunsho*, p. 386.

115. Kurusu to Baruch, July 7, 1947, Baruch MSS; also quoted in Kurusu, *Nichi Bei gaiko hiwa*, p. 175.

116. Quoted in Toland, *The Rising Sun*, p. 179. See also Morley, *Final Confrontation*, p. 319. For a more negative judgment, see Robert J. C. Butow, *Tojo and the Coming of the War* (Princeton, NJ: Princeton University Press, 1961), pp. 397-400.

117. Ballantine memorandum of conversation, November 18, 1941, *FRUS: Japan, 1931-41*, II, p. 745.

118. See Iguchi, *Demystifying*, ch. 21; see also Feis's cogent argument that the modus vivendi would likely have broken down in *Road to Pearl Harbor*, pp. 310-11.

119. Kido, quoted in Shigenori Tōgō, *The Cause of Japan* (New York: Simon & Schuster, 1956), p. 166.

120. Ibid.

121. Tōgō "treated the talks as his own and the diplomats in Washington as mere conduits for his orders." Hotta, *Japan 1941*, p. 259. Ironically, the same criticism was leveled at Grew when he strongly advocated a summit meeting between Roosevelt and Prime Minister Konoye in August-September 1941. Allegedly, "Grew had been in Japan too long . . . he was more Japanese than the Japanese." Stanley K. Hornbeck, quoted in George R. Packard, *Edwin O. Reischauer and the American Discovery of Japan* (New York: Columbia University Press, 2010), p. 66.

122. Quoted in Kato, *Lost War*, pp. 75-76.

123. On navy politics, see the recent essay by Peter Mauch, "The Dissembling Diplomat: Admiral Toyoda Teijiro and the Politics of Japanese Security," in Kimura and Minohara, eds., *Tumultuous Decade*, pp. 234-257.

124. Kurusu, *Homatsu*, pp. 200-02.

125. Kurusu to Baruch, July 7, 1947, Baruch MSS. Kurusu concluded, "By precipitating the Pearl Harbor attack, Japan chose war for peace, destruction for construction, economic ruination for prosperity."

126. Joseph C. Grew, *Ten Years in Japan* (New York: Simon & Schuster, 1944), p. 481.

127. Tadao Wikawa, quoted in Butow, *The John Doe Associates*, p. 293.

Kurusu's Preface

1. Nevile Henderson, *Failure of a Mission, 1937-1939* (London, 1940).

2. As late as 1953, Eleanor Roosevelt wrote to Nomura prior to her visit to Japan, "I know my husband always felt you had been honest with him. I remember his saying so. There were others he was not quite so sure about but I never heard him express a doubt about you." Eleanor Roosevelt to Kichisaburo Nomura, May 30, 1053, Box 1731, Eleanor Roosevelt MSS, FDRL.

Part I. Sketching on the Sand

1. Ambassador Joseph Grew similarly described his own efforts to avoid war in 1941 as "having been wiped out as if by a typhoon." Joseph Grew, *Ten Years in Japan* (New York: Simon & Schuster, 1944), p. x.

Chapter 1: The Interrupted, Misread, Misinterpreted Messages

1. Karuizawa today is a popular resort at the base of Mt. Asama, a little more than an hour's drive northwest of Tokyo.

2. Kurusu told a *New York Times* reporter that he resented being "called treacherous and double crossing by Americans. I have worked hard for peace. Now, in this war, I have lost everything—my reputation, my home, my only son. Let no one think I like war." *New York Times*, September 7, 1945. Kurusu's home had been destroyed by B-29s, and his only son, an aviator, had died in combat in 1945.

3. In a recent video interview, Kurusu's daughter Pia Kurusu White remembers visiting the bombed-out Kurusu family home in Tokyo immediately after the war. All that remained was a second-floor bathtub still hanging in the air, connected to water pipes.

Ashley A. White, Kurusu's great-great-grandaughter, shot the video as a high school project. https://www.youtube.com/watch?v=khThOQkh35w.

4. For a careful discussion of American cryptologists' errors in translating intercepted Japanese diplomatic messages, see Komatsu, *Importance of "Magic."*

5. Mitsumasa Yonai (1880-1948) was a career naval officer who also served briefly as prime minister in 1940.

6. For Terasaki's postwar efforts to protect Hirohito from indictment as a war criminal, see Jeans, *Terasaki*, ch. 6.

7. For a thorough discussion of this mistranslation of Dispatch #26, see Komatsu, *Importance of "Magic,"* pp. 295-300.

8. Saburo Kurusu to Bernard M. Baruch, July 7, 1947, Bernard Baruch MSS, Seeley Mudd Library, Princeton University, Princeton, New Jersey.

9. Bernard M. Baruch (1870-1965), financier and park-bench philosopher best known for directing the War Industries Board during World War I and for his role on the Atomic Energy Commission after World War II. See the scholarly biography by Jordan A. Schwarz, *The Speculator* (Chapel Hill: University of North Carolina Press, 1981).

Chapter 2: The Midnight Messenger

1. As early as August 4, 1941, Nomura had requested that Tōgō send a senior diplomat who was "well versed in affairs in and out of Japan" to assist him. He specifically named Kurusu as his preferred choice. See Mauch, *Sailor Diplomat*, p. 194.

2. As Tōgō explained in his memoirs, "The purpose of the sending of Kurusu, so far from being 'camouflage,' was to make the actual state of affairs [in Japan] known to the American government and to all those concerned. To refer to it as 'camouflage' is the merest nonsense." Tōgō, *The Cause of Japan*, p. 153.

3. Kurusu "spent the next twenty or so hours trying to acquaint himself with the 'informal conversations' held between Japan and the United States since the spring." Eri Hotta, *Japan 1941: Countdown to Infamy* (New York: Knopf, 2013), pp. 243-44.

4. See Robert Craigie, *Behind the Japanese Mask* (London and New York: Hutchinson, 1945), p. 130.

5. As Tōgō later recalled, he also told Kurusu, "In the event that the United States is interested in Plan A or Plan B, we should consider making some concessions." Quoted in James E. Morley, ed., *Japan's Road to the Pacific War: The Final Confrontation* (New York: Columbia University Press, 1994), p. 264.

6. Viscount Kikujiro Ishii (1866-1945) was Japan's foreign minister during World War I. As a special envoy to the United States, he negotiated the Lansing-Ishii Agreement, which temporarily eased tensions between the United States and Japan over China. During the 1930s, he opposed Japan's close ties with Germany and Italy. He was killed during a US fire-bombing of Tokyo in May 1945.

7. Eigo Fukai (1876-1945) was a Japanese banker as well as a member of Japan's delegations to the Paris Peace Conference (1919), the Washington Naval Conference (1921-1922), and the London Economic Conference (1933).

8. For Yoshida's efforts as ambassador to Great Britain, see J. W. Dower, *Empire and Aftermath: Yoshida Shigeru and the Japanese Experience, 1878-1954* (Cambridge, MA: Harvard University Press, 1079), pp. 141-188.

9. The previous foreign minister, Yōsuke Matsuoka, had recalled several ambassadors who "had foreign wives," although Kurusu had remained in Berlin until after

he had signed the Tripartite Pact. See David J. Lu, *Agony of Choice: Matsuoka Yosuke and the Rise and Fall of the Japanese Empire, 1880-1946* (Lanham, MD: Lexington Books, 2002), 148.

Chapter 3: My Meeting with Prime Minister Tōjō

1. *Hakama* are traditional Japanese clothing originally worn only by men on formal occasions but now used by both sexes. *Hakama* are tied to the waist and fall to the ankles in a loose fitting.

2. Teijirō Toyoda (1885-1961) replaced Yōsuke Matsuoka as foreign minister in July 1941. He was an admiral in the Japanese Imperial Navy who opposed the Tripartite Pact.

3. Tōjō's assumption that the United States would compromise rather than face a war in the Pacific was not without substance. The Roosevelt administration had committed itself to a "Europe First" strategy, naval incidents had already taken place in the North Atlantic between the US Navy and German U-boats, and Congress formally repealed the Neutrality Act while Kurusu was flying across the Pacific. US military leaders were pressing Hull and Roosevelt for more time to send B-17 bombers and other reinforcements to the Philippines.

4. A Shinto shrine in Tokyo, Japan, originally named Tokyo Shokon Sha, was built by the order of Emperor Meiji in 1869. It commemorates those who had died in the service of the Emperor dating back to 1853, sixteen years prior to the Meiji Restoration. According to Shinto doctrine, Yasukuni provides a permanent home to the souls of the fallen soldiers. Because Tōjō and other convicted war criminals are enshrined there, visits by Japanese leaders to Yasukuni remain controversial to the present day.

5. In an earlier draft, Kurusu quotes Tōjō as saying, "We shall never lose a battle at the beginning of war." Kurusu papers, National Diet Library, Tokyo.

6. Three days later, Tōjō told a subordinate in the Ministry of War, "Proposal B is not an excuse for war. I am praying to the Gods that somehow we will be able to get an agreement with the United States with this proposal." Quoted in Dower, *Empire and Aftermath*, 221.

7. Grew would later write of Kurusu in his own memoirs, "I had known Kurusu fairly intimately over many years. I had negotiated with him, played golf with him, played poker with him, and he, his American wife and charming daughter Jaye . . . had often been under our roof in Tokyo. Such close association helps one to size up any man. I have always regarded Kurusu as an intellectually honest man. I so regard him today." Joseph C. Grew, *Turbulent Era: A Diplomatic Record of Forty Years, 1904-1945* (Boston, 1952), p. 1378.

8. Alice Perry Grew was the grandniece of Commodore Matthew Perry, whose mission to Tokyo in 1853-54 had "opened" Japan to the world.

9. For Yoshida's efforts to prevent war in 1941, see Dower, *Empire and Aftermath*, pp. 216-26.

10. Based on an interview with Kurusu's widow Alice, historian John Toland describes the diplomat as having tiptoed into their bedroom late that night. "Where are you going?" she asked. "Probably to the United States," he said. After making him coffee and wrapping a steamer blanket around her husband, she insisted that their son Ryo accompany him on the first leg of his journey because "there was every pos-

sibility" that he might be assassinated. Toland, *The Rising Sun*, p. 165. Toland's notes of the interview are in Box 10, Toland MSS, FDRL.

11. Kurusu reportedly told his son, "Maybe I will not be able to come back. Look after the family." Quoted in Otto D. Tollischus, *Tokyo Record* (New York: Reynal and Hitchcock, 1943), p. 287.

Chapter 4: Passing through the Places of my Two Years of Service

1. Portugal, by remaining neutral, retained control over its nearby colony of Macau until the Japanese occupied it in 1943. In 1999, it became the last European colony to be restored to China.

2. Sayre would later write in his memoirs that he and Kurusu "had a long talk," and "from what he told me then I later felt convinced that he [Kurusu] was ignorant of any plans to attack Pearl Harbor." Francis B. Sayre, *Glad Adventure* (New York: Macmillan, 1957), p. 220.

3. Kurusu had been a consul in Chicago during World War I.

4. The *New York Times* correspondent in Manila quoted Kurusu as saying he was "going to Washington, but [I] have no great hopes for a successful conclusion to negotiations." US intelligence workers picked up Tokyo's rebuke of Kurusu for his public remarks a few days later. See Edwin T. Layton, *"And I Was There": Pearl Harbor and Midway—Breaking the Secrets* (Old Saybrook, CT: Konecky & Konecky, 2001), p. 189.

5. Kurusu refers to the Johnson-Reed Immigration Act of 1924, which effectively barred Asian immigration to the United States.

Chapter 5: My Forty-Eight Hours at Midway

1. Major James Devereaux later recalled that Kurusu had bought him several drinks at the island's only hotel. "I am going to Washington to see what I can do," said Kurusu. "I hope I can straighten out affairs and avoid trouble." Quoted in Bill Sloan, *Given Up for Dead: America's Heroic Stand at Wake Island* (New York: Bantam Books, 2008), p. 64.

2. William J. Keswick (1903-1990) had gained notoriety earlier in 1941 for operating an armored car, originally owned by the gangster Al Capone, to protect his company's assets in Shanghai before the Japanese took over the international settlement. See http://www.ecns.cn/experience/2013/08-07/76328.shtml.

3. Surprisingly, Kurusu does not mention that Father James E. Drought was a fellow passenger on the Clipper. This key member of the so-called John Doe Associates, who were attempting to facilitate negotiations between Tokyo and Washington, later recalled Kurusu telling him that "he had no message which would relieve the tension between his country and the United States, but only hoped to find some solution by hard work." Quoted in Butow, *John Doe Associates*, p. 438.

4. While Kurusu was traversing the Pacific, Churchill received a decryption of Kurusu's instructions that included the sentence "America would have to stop sending assistance to CHIANG KAI SHEK and instead would have to advise him to make peace." Churchill underlined that sentence in red. See Antony Best, *Britain, Japan, and Pearl Harbor: Avoiding War in East Asia* (London: Routledge, 1995), p. 180.

5. For a positive assessment of Craigie, see David Cameron Watt, *How War Came* (New York: Pantheon, 1989), pp. 54-55, 358-60.

6. For another possible opportunity for Japan and England to cooperate over China in this period, see Antony Best, "The Leith-Ross Mission and British Policy toward East Asia, 1934-7," *International History Review* 33 (Summer 2013), pp. 681-701.

7. Tetsuzan Nagata (1884-1935) was in charge of economic mobilization for Japan's Ministry of War. A moderate, he was assassinated in the notorious Aizawa Incident in August 1935 for allegedly putting the army "in the paws of high finance."

8. Enjiro Yamaza (1866–1914) was a decorated diplomat who was part of the Japanese delegation to assist Foreign Minister Jutaro Komura negotiate the Treaty of Portsmouth in 1905. He was appointed director of the Political Affairs Bureau in the Foreign Office at the young age of 36. His diplomatic stints included London, Beijing, and Seoul.

9. In Shanghai on August 26, 1937, a Japanese warplane machine-gunned the car of British ambassador Sir Hughe Knatchbull-Hugessen, wounding the ambassador. The Japanese government subsequently apologized.

10. See the detailed account of Yoshida's efforts in Ann Trotter, *Britain and East Asia, 1933-1937* (Cambridge, UK: Cambridge University Press, 1975), pp. 191-203.

11. See Mamoru Shigemitsu, *Japan and Her Destiny* (New York: Dutton, 1956), pp. 182-83.

12. For details of the Tientsin Incident, see Sebastian Swann, *Japan's Imperial Dilemma in China: The Tientsin Incident, 1939-1940* (London: Routledge, 2012).

13. One American Kurusu nearly encountered in Honolulu was Captain Ellis M. Zacharias, a former naval attaché to Japan who was then in command of the heavy cruiser USS *Salt Lake City*. Zacharias remembered Kurusu as the "husband of an American wife and father of a boy whom I used to bounce on my knee when he was a little lad." Because Kurusu had been a signatory to the Tripartite Pact, "a more flagrant violation of international etiquette and a more impertinent insult to the United States could hardly be imagined than to send a man to Washington to discuss peace who only a short while before had been the protagonist of an agreement spelling out war in capital letters." Nonetheless, Zacharias's efforts to meet with Kurusu "to learn something of his mission" came to naught. See Ellis M. Zacharias, *Secret Missions* (New York: Putnam's, 1946), pp. 234-35.

14. British journalist Alistair Cooke later recalled Kurusu's raucous first Washington press conference, in which the beleaguered diplomat finally pleaded to reporters, "This country is the land of liberty, as you call it. Please then, give me the liberty of silence." Alistair Cooke, *The American Home Front, 1941-1942* (London: Allen Lane, 2006), p. 3.

Chapter 6: Washington at the Time of My Arrival

1. Dispatch #646 from Nomura to Toyoda, dated August 4.

2. Dispatch #734 from Tōgō to Nomura, dated November 5.

3. Dispatch #1090 from Nomura to Tōgō, dated November 4.

4. Jutarō Komura (1855-1911), Japanese foreign minister during the Russo-Japanese War and Japan's chief delegate at the Portsmouth Peace Conference.

5. Hull later wrote that he felt "from the start that he [Kurusu] was deceitful. Knowing what I did of Japan's intentions from the intercepts . . . he was to lull us with talk until the moment Japan got ready to strike." *Memoirs*, II, pp. 1062-63.

Chapter 7: My First Meeting with the President

1. Dispatch #1118 from Nomura to Tōgō, dated November 17.

2. The U.S. record of the meeting quotes Kurusu as saying he had been "agreeably surprised when he discussed policies with General Tōjō and found him to be sincerely desirous of reaching an agreement with the United States." Ballantine memorandum of conversation, November 17, 1941, *FR: Japan, 1931-1941*, p. 738.

3. Marquess Shigenobu Okuma (1838-1922) was Japan's prime minister during the first two years of World War I.

4. Hull dismissed Kurusu's argument as "a specious attempt to explain away the Tripartite Pact." Hull memorandum, November 17, 1941, *FR: Japan, 1931-1941*, p. 740.

5. See John F. Bratzel, and Leslie B. Rout Jr., "FDR and the 'Secret Map,'" *The Wilson Quarterly* IX (January 1985), pp. 167-173.

6. That evening of November 17, Nomura and Kurusu met with Postmaster General Frank Walker, who told them, "The President is very desirous of an understanding between Japan and the United States. . . . If Japan should now do something real, such as evacuating French Indo-China, the way would be open for us to furnish you with oil and it would probably lead to the reestablishment of normal trade relations." Quoted in Morley, ed., *Final Confrontation*, p. 303.

Chapter 8: My First Negotiation with Hull

1. Dispatch #1131 from Nomura to Tōgō, dated November 16.

2. See the classic study by Paul W. Schroeder, *The Axis Alliance and Japanese-American Relations 1941* (Ithaca, NY: Cornell University Press, 1958).

3. Translators had mistranslated the instructions for Plan B "as a means of overcoming final barriers" to read instead as "our [Japanese] absolutely final proposal." Komatsu, *Importance of "Magic,"* p. 301.

4. Dispatch #1133 from Nomura to Tōgō, dated November 18.

5. Dispatch #798 from Tōgō to Nomura, dated November 20.

6. Tōgō stressed, "There is absolutely no room for maneuver." Quoted in Hotta, *Japan 1941*, p. 259.

Chapter 9: The Deteriorating One Week

1. According to the Japanese record, Kurusu asked Hull how he could reconcile his public stand for peace "with continued assistance to Chiang Kei-shek, which actually hinders peace." Quoted in Jonathan Marshall, *To Have and Have Not: Southeast Asian Raw Materials and the Origins of the Pacific War* (Berkeley: University of California Press, 1995), p. 150.

2. Kurusu's memorandum of his conversations with Hull quotes the secretary of state as saying, "Real politicians try to seek peace until the last minute." Kurusu Memo #11, November 22, 1941, Saburo Kurusu MSS, National Diet Library, Tokyo.

3. Hull said, "If the Japanese could not wait until Monday [November 24] before having his answer there was nothing he could do about it as he was obliged to confer again with the representatives of the other governments after they had had an opportunity to consult with their governments." Hull memorandum, November 22, 1941, *FRUS: Japan, 1931-1941*, II, p. 761.

4. Dispatch #821 from Tōgō to Nomura, dated November 24.
5. Dispatch #812 from Tōgō to Nomura, dated November 22.

Chapter 10: My Conference with Hull at His Home

1. Dispatch #1160 from Nomura to Tōgō, dated November 23.
2. For a careful argument that Hull was misled by several mistranslations on the part of interpreters that Japan would act "automatically" rather than "independently" under the Tripartite Pact, see Komatsu, *Importance of "Magic,"* pp. 307-09. For Kurusu's reluctant participation in the signing of the Tripartite Pact, see James W. Morley, ed., *Deterrent Diplomacy: Japan, Germany, and the USSR, 1935-1940* (New York: Columbia University Press, 1976), pp. 223-225, 228.
3. In Kurusu's unpublished chapter on the Tripartite Pact in September 1940, he wrote, "Immediately after the signing of the treaty, I sent in my resignation by wire. Considering the fact that I had not been in favor of this alliance and that it had been concluded secretly over my head, I had decided that I should not remain in office." He nonetheless stayed in Berlin until January 1941, when his successor, General Hiroshi Oshima, arrived. Kurusu MSS.
4. Dispatch #1160 from Nomura to Tōgō, dated November 23, and Dispatch #800 from Tōgō to Nomura, dated November 20.
5. As one scholar notes, the draft "virtually renounced Japan's obligations under the Tripartite Pact. If a peaceful understanding between Japan and the United States could be reached due to Kurusu's note, this would mean, objectively, that Japan would have abandoned the pact, and it would be all right for the note to be published and for Germany to learn of it. . . . Japan would be casting Germany aside, and choosing a path of cooperation with the United States." Seishiro Sugihara, *Between Incompetence and Culpability: Assessing the Diplomacy of Japan's Foreign Ministry from Pearl Harbor to Potsdam* (Lanham, MD: University Press of America, 1997), p. 46.
6. As a returning member of the Tokyo Embassy later put it, Kurusu was asking Hull not to insist on specific language renouncing the Tripartite Pact but "to read between the lines." John K. Emmerson, *The Japanese Thread* (New York: Holt, Rhinehart, and Winston, 1978), p. 120.
7. In his memoirs, Hull describes Kurusu's document as "merely" his "personal interpretation" and "so dismissed it." Hull, *Memoirs*, II, p. 1071.
8. Hull's memorandum of this meeting consists of four terse sentences with any hint of friendly conversation conspicuously absent. Hull memorandum, November 21, 1941, *Foreign Relations: Japan, 1931-1941*, II, p. 756.
9. In fact, Hull was secretly suffering from tuberculosis. See Gellman, *Secret Affairs*, pp. 31, 42, 266-67.

Chapter 11: Hull's Fatal Note

1. In his memoirs, Hull does not comment on the November 5 dispatch from Tōgō; he cites instead a cable on November 22 in which Tokyo changed the deadline for an agreement from November 25 to November 29. He quotes the translated dispatch: "This time we mean it, that the dead line absolutely cannot be changed. After that things are automatically going to happen." Hull, *Memoirs*, II, p. 1074.

Chapter 12: Negotiation Falls into a Tight Spot

1. Dispatches #1191, #1192, and #1193 from Nomura to Tōgō, dated November 27.
2. America's plan received from the secretary of state on November 26.
3. Dispatch #1193 from Nomura to Tōgō, dated November 26.
4. According to the US record, Kurusu noted that Japan's response to Hull's note "could be interpreted as tantamount to meaning the end." He asked about a modus vivendi, whereupon Hull said "we had explored that" with the other powers and "he had done his best in the way of exploration." Ballantine memorandum, November 26, 1941, *FR: Japan, 1931-1941*, II, p. 766.
5. Dispatch #1190 from Nomura to Tōgō, dated November 27.

Chapter 13: Our Second Meeting with the President

1. Dispatch #1190 from Nomura to Tōgō, dated November 27.
2. In fact, as the Australian minister reported, Hull "was depressed and upset by the turn of events. He blamed the Chinese principally for torpedoing of the modus vivendi." Casey to Evatt, cablegram 1045, November 27, 1941, http://www.dfat.gov.au/publications/historical/volume-05/historical-document-05-133.html.
3. Nomura had lost his right eye to a terrorist bomb while reviewing Japanese forces in Shanghai in May 1932.
4. According to Hull's record, Roosevelt used the phrase "a cold bath." Hull memorandum, November 27, 1941, *FR: Japan, 1931-1941*, II, p. 770. According to Nomura's diary, he said "cold water." Goldstein and Dillon, *Pacific War Papers*, p. 209.
5. Kurusu is correct. See Stimson Diary, November 26, 1941, and Stimson to Roosevelt, November 26, 1941, PSF War Department, FDRL.
6. See the classic account of attempted coups and assassinations by journalist Hugh Byas, *Government by Assassination* (New York: Knopf, 1942). See also Tetsuo Najita, *The Intellectual Origins of Modern Japanese Politics* (Chicago: University of Chicago Press, 1980), pp. 133-37.
7. According to Hull's memorandum of the conversation, it was he, not Kurusu, who "referred to 250,000 [Japanese] carpet-baggers" in northern China who "had seized other people's rights" just as "carpetbaggers had done in the south after the Civil War." Hull memorandum, November 27, 1941, *FR: Japan, 1931-1941*, p. 271.
8. According to Sir William Stephenson, the head of British secret intelligence in the United States, Roosevelt used his son James as a courier to pass on sensitive information. On November 26, after the Hull note, James Roosevelt informed the "man called Intrepid" that negotiations were "leading nowhere," whereupon the following cable went to Winston Churchill: "JAPANESE NEGOTIATIONS OFF. SERVICES EXPECT ACTION WITHIN TWO WEEKS." William Stevenson, *A Man Called Intrepid* (New York: Harcourt Brace Jovanovich, 1976), p. 299.
9. "All United States efforts to solve differences with Japan appeared exhausted yesterday, and the next move—either diplomatic or military—seemed up to Tokyo." *New York Times*, November 28, 1941.

Chapter 14: Prime Minister Tōjō's Speech to Expel America and Great Britain

1. Dispatch #844 from Tōgō to Nomura, dated November 26.

2. Dispatch #857 from Tōgō to Nomura, dated November 30.

3. In Hull's memoir, he again notes that Nomura and Kurusu were trying to "lull us with talk until the moment the Japanese military were ready to strike." *Memoirs*, II, pp. 1087-88.

4. Dispatch #1222 Nomura to Tōgō, dated November 30.

5. Dispatch #866 from Tōgō, to Nomura, dated December 1.

6. See also statement of Hidenari Terasaki, first secretary at the Japanese Embasssy, to Ballantine, December 2, 1941, *FR: Japan, 1931-1941*, II, p. 778.

7. Dispatch #1225 from Nomura to Tōgō, dated December 1.

8. Hull said "he has heard not one whisper of peace from the Japanese military, only bluster and blood-curdling threats." Ballantine memorandum of conversation, December 1, 1941, *FR: Japan, 1931-1941*, II, p. 775.

9. According to the US version, Kurusu said, "If we don't look out China will sell both the United states and Japan down the river." Ibid., II, p. 776.

Chapter 15: The Plan for the Exchange of Messages between the Heads of State

1. The English text Keenan showed Kurusu was a mistranslation and misreading of this cable.

2. Kurusu's concern here may have been influenced by the occupation of Dutch Guiana (Suriname) by US troops on November 24 at the invitation of the Dutch government-in-exile. Japan, of course, had already occupied all of French Indochina by late July.

3. Dispatch #1180 from Nomura to Tōgō, dated November 26.

4. In his memoirs, Tōgō quotes Kido saying that "such a plan would result in rebellion." Tōgō, *The Cause of Japan*, p. 166.

5. In his final report, Kurusu obscured the embassy's responsibility for Roosevelt's message to Hirohito. He wrote, "Independent from us, there were two groups—one, Senator Thomas and his collaborators, and two, Reverend E. Stanley Jones and other Christians—that were trying to influence the President with their plans to exchange cables, there was no way of stopping them. And we learned that the cable from the president was eventually dispatched. I suspect it was probably related to aforementioned Senator Thomas's or Reverend Jones' original plan." Kurusu Final Report, June 2, 1942, Gaimusho, *Nihon Gaiko Bunsho*, p. 384. For Thomas's involvement, see Haruo Iguchi, "Senator Elbert Thomas and Japan," *Journal of American & Canadian Studies* 27 (2007), pp. 81-83.

6. Dispatch #1227 from Nomura to Tōgō, dated December 1.

7. British intelligence chief Sir William Stephenson told Air Attaché Roald Dahl (later a famous author of children's stories) that his agents had "bugged the hotel room of Saburo Kurusu" when he arrived in Washington" and "the exact date of the Pearl Harbor attack had been mentioned in these taped conversations." Stephenson allegedly forwarded these transcripts to Roosevelt, who did nothing. Dahl did not believe the story, nor should historians, because Kurusu did not stay at a hotel, and he did not know about the pending attack on Pearl Harbor. See Donald Sturbrock, *Storyteller: The Authorized Biography of Roald Dahl* (New York: Simon & Schuster, 2010), p. 210n.

8. Casey had already warned Washington officials about the danger of "pinpricks and provocation" that might push Japan into launching a preemptive attack. Quoted in Richard J. Aldrich, *Intelligence and the War against Japan* (New York: Cambridge University Press, 2000), p. 89.

9. As Casey reported to his government, "Kurusu was very friendly and informal and showed every desire for a peaceful solution. He deprecated the belligerent speeches of Japanese statesmen and minimized Japan's Axis connection. He laughed at the statements by Japanese politicians of the 'encirclement' of Japan by the Americans and British. He blamed China for the virtual breakdown in the conversations with the United States and said that the present situation appeared to mean that the issue of war and peace in the Pacific rested solely in the hands of China. I suggested that an important factor . . . lay in the fact that during the conversations between himself and the Secretary of State, Japan had been formidably increasing her forces in Southern Indo-China. Kurusu professed ignorance of this. . . . Kurusu had no proposal to make other than that discussions on the limited Japanese proposal be resumed." Casey to Evatt, Cablegram 1055, November 30, 1941, http://www.dfat.gov.au/publications/historical/volume-05/historical-document-05-144.html.

10. In fact, as Casey reported, Hull opposed any meeting between Halifax and Kurusu: "The Secretary of State cannot see any advantage in the British Ambassador seeing Kurusu. The British Ambassador tends to agree with this. It is unlikely that Kurusu would have any viewpoint to put forward that he did not put to me and if by a bad chance such a meeting became known publicly, much damage might be done." Casey to Evatt, Cablegram 1057, November 30, 1941, http://www.dfat.gov.au/publications/historical/volume-05/historical-document-05-146.html.

11. Halifax did in fact encourage Roosevelt to send a message to the emperor. "As to the treatment of Kurusu's approach generally," he cabled London on December 5, "I said no doubt he [Roosevelt] would be particularly careful not to put a foot wrong with the Chinese after last week's experience, and that therefore it would be wiser to avoid any detailed suggestion at first stage merely combining with message and warning, a hint that if Emperor's reply gave him any reason to think it would be helpful, he might be able to make a suggestion that would assist in the maintenance of peaceful relations. The President agreed." Halifax to Foreign Office, #5603, December 5, 1941, FO371/27914, British Public Record Office, Kew, England.

12. According to Davies's diary, Kurusu again urged that Roosevelt send a cable to Hirohito as the only means of avoiding war. See diary of Joseph E. Davies, November 28, 1941, Joseph E. Davies MSS, Library of Congress.

Chapter 16: The "If" Lurking behind History

1. Stanley Jones sent a heartfelt letter to Kurusu after the Pearl Harbor attack in which he expressed his appreciation for Kurusu's tireless work. The Kurusu Collection, The National Diet Library, Tokyo, Japan.

2. For Walsh and Drought, see the definitive study by Butow, *John Doe Associates.*

3. Part of the difficulty was that the John Doe Associates had actually drawn up the proposals that Nomura had had misreported as an American plan. As Marius Jansen writes, "The result was confusion over what was and what was not the 'Tokyo' position, with Washington formulating responses to proposals that had never been

authentic, heightening distrust and suspicion." Marius B. Jansen, *The Making of Modern Japan* (Cambridge, MA: Harvard University Press, 2000), p. 634.

4. See E. Stanley Jones, "An Adventure in Failure: Behind the Scenes Before Pearl Harbor," *Asia and the Americas* 45 (December 1945), pp. 609-16.

5. Jones wrote the following to Kurusu four days after Pearl Harbor, "Thank you for your valiant efforts for peace. You have failed, but you have the satisfaction of knowing that you did your level best to bring these two nations together. The failure is not yours! It is the failure of those who did not want peace as you did." Jones to Kurusu, December 11, 1941, Kurusu MSS.

Chapter 17: The Kindness of Baruch

1. In Kurusu's papers in Tokyo is an article from the *Nippon Times*, dated June 18, 1950, that quotes Bernard M. Baruch affirming that Kurusu was "a good man who did his best to stop the war." Kurusu MSS.

2. Kurusu did not know that Desvernine was consulting with former president Herbert Hoover. It was Hoover who suggested enlisting Bernard M. Baruch as the intermediary who would bypass the State Department and approach both Kurusu and Roosevelt in reviving a modus vivendi. See J. Garry Clifford and Masako Rachel Okura, "Side Door Diplomacy: Herbert Hoover, FDR, and United States-Japanese Negotiations, 1941," *Peace & Change* XXXVIII (April 2013), pp. 207-236.

3. Other sources indicate that the Kurusu-Baruch meeting took place at the Mayflower Hotel on December 1. See Clifford and Okura, "Side Door Diplomacy," p. 217.

4. This is a reference to the Nomonhan Incident, which occurred in August 1939, when Soviet forces commanded by General Georgii Zhukov routed Japanese forces along the Manchurian-Mongolian border. In his recent book *Nomonhan, 1939* (Annapolis, MD: Naval Institute Press, 2012), Stuart D. Goldman argues that the Japanese commander who instigated the border clash, Tsuji Masanobu, later persuaded his superiors not to go to war with the Soviet Union in 1941 but to attack the United States and England instead.

5. With his insider connections, Baruch may well have learned of the proposal by US Treasury official Harry Dexter White to offer a twenty-year $2 billion credit to Japan as part of a sweeping attempt to avoid war in the Pacific. White's plan never became official. See David Rees, *Harry Dexter White: A Study in Paradox* (New York: Coward, McCann & Geoghegan, 1973), pp. 122-23. After the war, Kurusu told a friend that he regarded Baruch's proposal for a billion-dollar loan to Japan as a "million-to-one opportunity" that had "slipped through [his] hands" because of Pearl Harbor. Quoted in Haruo Iguchi, *Unfinished Business: Ayukawa Yoshisuke and U.S.-Japanese Relations, 1937-1953* (Cambridge, MA: Harvard University Press, 2003), p. 170.

Chapter 18: The Final Ultimatum

1. Dispatch #879 from Tojo to Nomura, dated December 3.

2. The US memo of the meeting quotes Kurusu as saying that "the reaction which has been caused in Japan by [the US] freezing order. . . produces a frame of mind which has to be taken into account." Ballantine memo of conversation, December 2, 1941, *Foreign Relations: Japan, 1931-1941*, II, p. 780.

3. American proposal received from the secretary of state on June 21, 1941.

4. Japanese proposal handed to Ballantine by Secretary Matsudaira on September 27, 1941 (counterproposal to the American plan of June 21).

5. According to the American counselor to the Japanese Embassy, Kurusu showed some bitterness that Welles, sitting "in his comfortable easy chair with nothing personally to worry about," was "unable to realize the sufferings of others." He quoted Welles "with a touch of scorn as saying that 'the United States should not sell China down the river' and suggested that the undersecretary of state might give some consideration to the Japanese people." Frederick Moore, *With Japan's Leaders* (New York: Scribner's, 1942), pp. 280-81.

6. Dispatch #875 from Tōgō to Nomura, dated December 2.

7. In Tokyo, Admiral Matome Ugaki, the chief of staff of Japan's Combined Fleet, reacted to the US query by noting in his diary, "Don't you know that a dagger will be thrust into your throat in four days?" *Fading Victory: The Diary of Admiral Matome Ugaki, 1941-1945* (Pittsburgh: University of Pittsburgh Press, 1991), p. 35.

8. Dispatch #1256 from Nomura to Tōgō, dated December 3.

9. Dispatch #891 from Tōgō to Nomura, dated December 4.

10. Kurusu pleaded, "If we could only come to an agreement on temporary measures we could then proceed with our exploration of fundamental solutions. . . . [A] fundamental agreement would necessarily take time and . . . what was needed was a temporary expedient." Ballantine memo of conversation, December 5, 1941, *FR: Japan, 1931-1941*, II, p. 783.

11. For the problems of translation and transcription that delayed the Japanese presentation of their final note on December 7, see Robert J. C. Butow, "Marching off on the Wrong Foot: The Final Note Tokyo Did Not Send to Washington," *Pacific Historical Review* LXIII (February 1994), pp. 67-79. For Japanese perspectives, see Naraichi Fujiyama, *Ichi Seinen Gaikokan no Taiheiyo Senso* (1989), pp. 80-95, and "Nichibeikaisen Zenya no Zaibei Taishikan" *Gaiko Shiryo Kampo*, Ministry of Foreign Affairs (1991:4), pp. 27-43. Fujiyama was one of the embassy staffers who decoded the fateful telegram from Japan.

12. The Japanese government's reply was transmitted to the secretary of state at 2 p.m. on December 7, 1941.

13. One account, citing eyewitnesses, claims that Hull expressed in clear Tennessee "mountainese" his doubts about "the paternity of Messrs. Nomura and Kurusu," whereupon the two envoys departed "wild-eyed and really scared." Kurusu's recollection is similar to Hull's. See Helen Lombard, *While They Fought* (New York: Scribner's, 1947), p. 11. British journalist Alistair Cooke also notes, "Cordell Hull was bred in the mountains of Tennessee, and there is nobody alive who in anger more notably retraces his spiritual ancestry. . . . Mr. Hull is capable of an abusive idiom, deriving half from animal biology, half from the Bible. . . . Let us hope that Mr. Kurusu, who is so adept at the English language, heard rolling periods that staggered him, and hissing, toothy phrases he will never forget even if he will never know a place to repeat them." Cooke, *American Home Front, 1941-1942*, p. 9.

14. Nomura wrote in his diary, "FBI began strict surveillance from today and we began a life of confinement." Goldstein and Dillon, *Pacific War Papers*, p. 213.

15. Kurusu's stunned reaction was echoed across the Atlantic by British diplomat Oliver Hardy: "We're all astounded by Japan. . . . We never thought she would attack us and America at once. She must have gone mad." Quoted in Christopher Thorne, *The Issue of War* (New York: Oxford University Press, 1985), p. 10.

Chapter 19: Life during Internment

1. US authorities worried that Nomura might commit suicide, which they feared would endanger American diplomats interned in Japan. Nomura implied that he would not take his own life. See entry of December 13, 1941, in Fred L. Israel, ed., *The War Diary of Breckinridge Long* (Lincoln: University of Nebraska Press, 1966), p. 229.

2. Fumitaka Konoye (1915-1956), the eldest son of Prime Minister Fumimaro Konoye, was an avid amateur golfer. He studied at Princeton, and after the war ended in August 1945, the Soviet Army captured him, along with more than half a million Japanese soldiers left behind in Manchuria. Despite repeated pleas from the Japanese government, he was never released from a POW camp. His remains were returned to his family in 1958, two years after the Soviet Union and Japan re-established diplomatic relations.

3. Interned Japanese journalist Masuo Kato had played golf at the Homestead previously. He was told, however, that golf was not permitted because "there were a number of people in the district obsessed with a desire to shoot Japanese on sight, and therefore golfing might come under the heading of hazardous occupations." Masuo Kato, *The Lost War* (New York: Knopf, 1946), p. 69. Ironically, despite the difficult six-month internment endured by American diplomats in the US Embassy in Tokyo, Ambassador Grew kept morale high by setting up "a Greater East Asia Co-Prosperity Golf Course inside the compound, a nine-hole 422-yard, pitch-and-putt affair with the swimming pool and reflecting pond only the most obvious hazards." Waldo H. Heinrichs Jr., *American Ambassador: Joseph C. Grew and the Development of the American Diplomatic Tradition* (Boston: Little, Brown, 1966), p. 359.

4. By April 1942, Nomura had to warn Japanese internees that "they were eating too much and too well" and suggested that "they would have a shock upon their arrival in Japan at the food condition." Quoted in Mauch, *Sailor Diplomat*, p. 215.

5. For the importance of baseball to Japanese-American relations, see the wonderful book by Sayuri Guthrie-Shimizu, *Transpacific Field of Dreams: How Baseball Linked the United States and Japan in Peace and War* (Chapel Hill: University of North Carolina Press, 2012).

6. In comparison to the relatively "plush" quarters at the Greenbrier for Japanese internees, US diplomats in Japan referred to their own cramped spaces as "Black Sulphur Springs." Jeans, *Terasaki*, p. 157.

7. The Axis internees did not coexist easily. The ranking German diplomat, Hans Thomsen, had to give "orders to Germans not to criticize the Japanese and to treat them nice at all times." Quoted in Mauch, *Sailor Diplomat*, p. 250.

8. For a thorough study of internment and repatriation, see P. Scott Corbett, *Quiet Passages: The Exchange of Civilians between the United States and Japan during the Second World War* (Kent, OH: Kent State University Press, 1987).

Chapter 20: Several Speculations

1. Perhaps the best study of Japanese foreign policy between the two world wars is by Ian Nish, *Japanese Foreign Policy in the Interwar Period* (Westport, CT: Praeger, 2002).

2. Proposal of Japanese-American Understanding, for which instructions were asked on April 17, 1941.

3. What Kurusu calls the "American proposal" of April 1941 was actually a proposal drawn up by the John Doe Associates, not the US government. Hull thought the terms were proposed by Tokyo, and Nomura confused his own government by referring to it as an American plan. See Robert J. C. Butow, "The Hull-Nomura Conversations: A Fundamental Misconception," *American Historical Review* LXV (July 1960), pp. 822-836.

4. Following Japan's occupation of southern French Indochina, Washington instituted an oil embargo that "had a tremendous psychological impact upon the Japanese. The ambivalence and ambiguities in their perception of world events disappeared, replaced by a sense of clear-cut alternatives." Akira Iriye, *Power and Culture: The Japanese-American War, 1941-1945* (Cambridge, MA: Harvard University Press, 1981), p. 28.

5. In a speech on November 26, 1942, Kurusu suggested another motive: "According to information that reached my ears at the time, not a few. . . in the United States believed that the best method of unifying without dissent the American views on American entry into the war, which were then suffering a growing split, would be to drive Japan into a tight corner and force the start of a Pacific war." *Kurusu Speaks* (Tokyo: Nippon Times Ltd., 1944), p. 11.

Chapter 21: Contemplation and Observation

1. Attack upon Pearl Harbor by Japanese armed forces: Report of the commission appointed by the President of the United States to investigate and report the facts relating to the attack made by Japanese armed forces upon Pearl Harbor in the Territory of Hawaii on December 7, 1941. Print: Gov. Docs; SERIAL-SET-ID: 10676 S.doc 159.

2. Roy L. Morgan (1908-1985) was an attorney and FBI agent who oversaw the detention of Axis diplomats in the United States in 1941-42. He later served as the associate counsel and chief of the Investigative Division of the International Prosecution Section of the International Military Tribunal for the Far East in 1946.

Chapter 22: Exchange Ship

1. For further details on the wartime voyages of the *Gripsholm* in repatriating internees, see http://www.salship.se/mercy.asp.

2. According to an eyewitness, Nomura had sent a message to Grew requesting a meeting, but Grew had declined. Nomura reportedly said, "Oh well, he's a diplomat. I'm just an honest old sailor." Quoted in Tollischus, *Tokyo Record*, p. 396.

3. Count Hisaichi Terauchi (1879-1946) served as Japan's minister of war in 1936-1937 and commanded the Southern Expeditionary Army Group, which captured Singapore and conquered Southeast Asia in 1942. He died of a stroke while a prisoner of war in 1946.

4. According to Eri Hotta, "This was a chilling and disheartening revelation for Kurusu. That the military leaders *had*, in fact, decided for war by November 26 confirmed that he and Nomura were told to continue diplomacy in a deliberate attempt to deceive and mislead the other side." Hotta, *Japan 1941*, p. 281.

Chapter 23: Arrival Home

1. It should be noted that Kurusu's final report carefully played down the role that he and Taro Terasaki, the Japanese embassy's first secretary, had played in using Jones and Baruch as intermediaries who urged Roosevelt's last-minute message to Hirohito. Kurusu wrote, "Although I heard that independent from us, there were two groups—one, Senator [Elbert] Thomas and his collaborators, and two, Reverend E. Stanley Jones and other Christians—that were trying to influence the President with their plans to exchange cables, there was no way of stopping them. And we learned that the cable from the president was eventually dispatched. I suspect it was probably related to aforementioned Senator Thomas's or Reverend Jones's original plan." Kurusu's Final Report, June 2, 1942, Gaimusho, *Nihon Gaikô Bunsho*, II, p. 384.

2. Prince Nobuhito Takamatsu (1905-1987), a younger brother of Hirohito's who served as an officer in the Japanese Imperial Navy. He opposed Japan's expansionist policies in the 1930s and urged early negotiations for peace after Japan's defeat at Midway in 1942.

3. For Takamatsu's eleventh-hour efforts to oppose war in 1941, see Marquis Kōichi Kido diary, November 30, 1941, in Goldstein and Dillon, eds., *Pacific War Papers*, pp. 133-34.

4. Munemitsu Mutsu (1844-1897) and Jutarō Komura (1855-1911) were Japanese diplomats during the Meiji era.

5. For an excellent recent study of US-Japanese relations from the 1890s through 1941, see Sidney Pash, *The Currents of War: A New History of American-Japanese Relations, 1899-1941* (Lexington: University Press of Kentucky, 2014).

6. For Tōjō's policy toward East Asia at this time, see Iriye, *Power and Culture*, pp. 67-72; see also Thorne, *Issue of War*, pp. 113-15.

7. For Oshima's report of his last conference with Adolf Hitler, on September 4, 1944, see Carl Boyd, *The Extraordinary Envoy* (Washington, DC: University Press of America, 1980), pp. 185-190.

8. Even as ambassador to Germany in 1940, Kurusu had maintained informal contacts with the Chinese Nationalist ambassador in Berlin. James W. Morley, ed., *The China Quagmire: Japan's Expansion on the Asian Continent, 1933-1941* (New York: Columbia University Press, 1983), p. 417.

9. For an excellent summary of the abortive Konoye peace mission, see Tsuyoshi Hasegawa, *Racing the Enemy: Stalin, Truman, and the Surrender of Japan* (Cambridge, MA: Harvard University Press, 2005), pp. 120-26, 143-45.

Bibliography

Books and Articles

Aldrich, Richard J. *Intelligence and the War against Japan*. London: Cambridge University Press, 2000.

Aldrich, Richard J. "Conspiracy or Confusion: Churchill, Roosevelt, and Pearl Harbor." *Intelligence and National Security* 7:3 (1992).

Aldrich, Richard J. *The Key to the South*. London: Oxford University Press, 1993.

Australian Government, Department of Foreign Affairs and Trade. *Documents on Australian Foreign Policy*, http://www.dfat.gov.au/publications/historical/volume-05/historical-document-95-140.html

Baruch, Bernard M. *Baruch: The Public Years: My Own Story*. New York: Holt, Rinehart and Winston, 1960.

Berle, Beatrice Bishop, and Jacobs, Travis Beal, eds. *Navigating the Rapids, 1918-1971: From the Papers of Adolf A. Berle*. New York: Harcourt Brace Jovanovich, 1973.

Best, Antony. *Britain, Japan, and Pearl Harbor: Avoiding War in East Asia*. London: Routledge, 1995.

Best, Antony. "The Leith-Ross Mission and British Policy toward East Asia, 1934-7." *International History Review* Summer 2013.

Best, Gary Dean. *Herbert Hoover: The Postpresidential Years, 1933-1964*. 2 vols. Stanford, CA: Hoover Institution Press, 1973.

Bix, Herbert P. *Emperor Hirohito and the Making of Modern Japan*. New York: Harper Collins, 2000.

Boyd, Carl. *Hitler's Japanese Confidant*. Lawrence: University of Kansas Press, 1993.

Boyd, Carl. *The Extraordinary Envoy*. Washington, DC: University Press of America, 1980.

Bratzel, John F., and Rout, Leslie B. Jr. "FDR and the 'Secret Map.'" *The Wilson Quarterly* January 1985.

Bridge, Carl, ed. *A Delicate Mission: The Washington Diaries of R. G. Casey, 1940-42*. Canberra: National Library of Australia, 2008.

Bowie, Theodore, ed. *Langdon Warner Through His Letters*. Bloomington: Indiana University Press, 1966.

Butow, Robert J. C. "Marching off on the Wrong Foot: The Final Note Tokyo Did Not Send to Washington." *Pacific Historical Review* February 1994.

Butow, Robert J. C. "Pearl Harbor Jitters." *Prologue* Winter 1991.

Butow, Robert J. C. "The Hull-Nomura Conversations: A Fundamental Misconception." *American Historical Review* July 1960.

Butow, Robert J. C. *The John Doe Associates: Backdoor Diplomacy for Peace, 1941.* Stanford, CA: Stanford University Press, 1974.

Butow, Robert J. C. *Tojo and the Coming of the War.* Princeton, NJ: Princeton University Press, 1961.

Byas, Hugh. *Government by Assassination.* New York: Knopf, 1942.

Clifford, J. Garry, and Okura, Masako Rachel. "Side Door Diplomacy: Herbert Hoover, FDR, and United States-Japanese Negotiations, 1941." *Peace & Change* April 2013.

Cooke, Alistair. *The American Home Front, 1941-1942.* London: Allen Lane, 2006.

Corbett, Scott P. *Quiet Passages: The Exchange of Civilians between the United States and Japan during the Second World War.* Kent, OH: Kent State University Press, 1987.

Craigie, Robert. *Behind the Japanese Mask.* London and New York: Hutchinson, 1945.

Dallek, Robert. *Franklin Roosevelt and American Foreign Policy, 1932-1945.* New York: Oxford University Press, 1979.

Dower, John W. *Empire and Aftermath: Yoshida Shigeru and the Japanese Experience, 1878-1954.* Cambridge, MA: Harvard University Press, 1979.

Dower, John W. *War Without Mercy: Race and Power in the Pacific War.* New York: Pantheon, 1987.

Emmerson, John K. *The Japanese Thread.* New York: Holt, Rhinehart, and Winston, 1978.

Feis, Herbert. *The Road to Pearl Harbor: The Coming of the War Between the United States and Japan.* New York: Atheneum, 1967.

Fleisher, Wilfred. *Our Enemy Japan.* Garden City, NY: Doubleday, 1942.

Fujiyama, Naraichi. *Ichi Seinen Gaikokan no Taiheiyo Senso.* Tokyo: Shinchosha, 1989.

Fujiyama, Naraichi. "Nichibei Zenya no Zaibei Taishikan" *Gaiko Shiryo Kampo.* Ministry of Foreign Affairs (1991:4)

Gaimusho (Japanese Ministry of Foreign Affairs), ed. *Nihon Gaikô Bunsho: Nichi-Bei Kôshô, 1941.* 2 vols. Tokyo: Gaimusho, 1990.

Gallichio, Mark. *The African American Encounter with Japan and China.* Chapel Hill: University of North Carolina Press, 2000.

Gellman, Irwin. *Secret Affairs.* Baltimore, MD: Johns Hopkins University Press, 1995.

Goldman, Stuart D. *Nomonhan, 1939.* Annapolis, MD: Naval Institute Press, 2012.

Goldstein, Donald M., and Dillon, Katherine D., eds. *Fading Victory: The Diary of Admiral Matome Ugaki, 1941-1945.* Pittsburgh: University of Pittsburgh Press, 1991.

Goldstein, Donald M., and Dillon, Katherine D., eds. *The Pacific War Papers.* Washington, DC: Potomac, 2004.

Grew, Joseph C. *Ten Years in Japan*. New York: Simon & Schuster, 1944.

Grew, Joseph C. *Turbulent Era: A Diplomatic Record of Forty Years, 1904-1945*. Boston: Houghton Mifflin, 1952.

Guthrie-Shimizu, Sayuri. *Transpacific Field of Dreams: How Baseball Linked the United States and Japan in Peace and War*. Chapel Hill: University of North Carolina Press, 2012.

Hasegawa, Tsuyoshi. *Racing the Enemy: Stalin, Truman, and the Surrender of Japan*. Cambridge, MA: Harvard University Press, 2005.

Heinrichs, Waldo H. Jr. *American Ambassador: Joseph C. Grew and the Development of the American Diplomatic Tradition*. Boston: Little, Brown, 1966.

Henderson, Nevile, *Failure of a Mission, 1937-1939*. New York: Putnam's, 1940.

Hoehling, A. A. *The Week Before Pearl Harbor*. New York: Norton, 1963.

Hogan, Michael J. ed., *Paths to Power: The Historiography of American Foreign Relations to 1941*. New York: Cambridge University Press, 2000.

Horne, Gerald. *Race War*. New York: New York University Press, 2005.

Hotta, Eri. *Japan 1941: Countdown to Infamy*. New York: Knopf, 2013.

Hsu, Immanuel C. Y. "Kurusu's Mission to the United States and the Abortive *Modus Vivendi*," *Journal of Modern History* September 1952.

Hull, Cordell. *The Memoirs of Cordell Hull*. 2 vols. New York: Macmillan, 1948.

Iguchi, Haruo. "Herbert C. Hoover Moto Daitoryō to Nichibei Sensō: Shinjuwan Chokuzen no Hoover Nikki no Shinpyōsei" [Behind-the-Scenes Herbert C. Hoover's Involvement in and Account of U.S.-Japan Diplomacy Right Before Japan's Pearl Harbor Attack]. *Doshisha Amerika kenkyū* March 1999.

Iguchi, Haruo. "Senator Elbert D. Thomas and Japan." *Journal of American & Canadian Studies* 25 (2007).

Iguchi, Haruo. *Unfinished Business: Ayukawa Yoshisuke and U.S.-Japanese Relations, 1937-1953*. Cambridge: Harvard University Press, 2003.

Iguchi, Takeo. *Demystifying Pearl Harbor*. Tokyo: International House of Japan, 2009.

Iriye, Akira. *Power and Culture: The Japanese-American War, 1941-1945*. Cambridge: Harvard University Press, 1981.

Israel, Fred L., ed. *The War Diary of Breckinridge Long*. Lincoln: University of Nebraska Press, 1966.

Jansen, Marius. *The Making of Modern Japan*. Cambridge: Harvard University Press, 2000.

Jeans, Roger. *Terasaki Hidenari, Pearl Harbor, and Occupied Japan: A Bridge to Reality*. New York: Lexington, 2009.

Jones, E. Stanley. "An Adventure in Failure: Behind the Scenes Before Pearl Harbor." *Asia and the Americas* December 1945.

Jones, F. C. *Japan's New Order in East Asia: Its Rise and Fall, 1937-45*. New York: Oxford University Press, 1954.

Kato, Masuo. *The Lost War: A Japanese Reporter's Inside Story*. New York: Knopf, 1946.

Kawamura, Noriko. "Emperor Hirohito and Japan's Decision to Go to War with the United States Reexamined." *Diplomatic History* January 2007.

Kimura, Masato, and Tosh Minohara, eds. *Tumultuous Decade: Empire, Society, and Diplomacy in 1930s Japan*. Toronto: University of Toronto Press, 2013.

Komatsu, Keiichiro. *Origins of the Pacific War and the Importance of "Magic."* London: Routledge, 2009.

Kurusu, Saburo. *Hōmatsu no sanjūgonen*. Tokyo, 1948.

Kurusu, Saburo. *Kurusu Speaks*. Tokyo: Nippon Times Ltd., 1944.

Kurusu, Saburo. *Nichi-Bei gaikō hiwa*. Tokyo: Sogensha, 1952.

Langer, William L., and Gleason S. Everett, *The Undeclared War, 1940-1941*. New York: Harper & Row, 1952.

Lawrence, Neal Henry. "The Unforgettable Alice J. Kurusu," http://www.asjapan.org/web.php/lectures/2000/05.

Layton, Edwin T. *"And I was There": Pearl Harbor and Midway—Breaking the Secrets*. Old Saybrook, CT: Konecky & Konecky, 2001.

Lomazow, Steven, and Eric Fetmann. *FDR's Deadly Secret*. New York: Public Affairs, 2009.

Lombard, Helen. *While They Fought*. New York: Scribner's, 1947.

Love, Robert W. Jr., ed. *Pearl Harbor Revisited*. New York: St. Martin's, 1995.

Lu, David J. *Agony of Choice: Matsuoka Yosuke and the Rise and Fall of the Japanese Empire, 1880-1946*. Lanham, MD: Lexington Books, 2002.

Lu, David J. *From the Marco Polo Bridge to Pearl Harbor*. Washington, DC: Public Affairs, 1961.

Marshall, Jonathan. *To Have and Have Not: Southeast Asian Raw Materials and the Origins of the Pacific War*. Berkeley: University of California Press, 1995.

Mauch, Peter. "Revisiting Nomura's Diplomacy: Ambassador Nomura's Role in the Japanese-American Negotiation, 1941." *Diplomatic History* June 2004.

Mauch, Peter. *Sailor Diplomat*. Cambridge, MA: Harvard University Press, 2011.

Mawdsley, Evan. *December 1941: Twelve Days that Began a World War*. New Haven, CT: Yale University Press, 2011.

Mayers, David. *FDR's Ambassadors and the Diplomacy of Crisis*. New York: Cambridge University Press, 2013.

Morley, James W. ed. *The China Quagmire: Japan's Expansion on the Asian Continent, 1933-1941*. New York: Columbia University Press, 1983.

Morley, James W., ed. *Deterrent Diplomacy: Japan, Germany, and the USSR, 1935-1940*. New York: Columbia University Press, 1976.

Morley, James E., ed. *Japan's Road to the Pacific War: The Final Confrontation*. New York: Columbia University Press, 1994.

Moore, Frederick. *With Japan's Leaders*. New York: Scribner's, 1942.

Najita, Tetsuo. *The Intellectual Origins of Modern Japanese Politics*. Chicago: University of Chicago Press, 1980.

Nash, George H., ed. *Freedom Betrayed: Herbert Hoover's Secret History of World War II and Its Aftermath*. Stanford, CA: Hoover Institution Press, 2011.

Nish, Ian. *Japanese Foreign Policy in the Interwar Period*. Westport, CT: Praeger, 2002.

O. C. "The Guilty: Saburo Kurusu," *Collier's Weekly* June 24, 1944.

Packard, George R. *Edwin O. Reischauer and the American Discovery of Japan.* New York: Columbia University Press, 2010.

Pash, Sidney. *The Currents of War: A New History of American-Japanese Relations, 1899-1941*. Lexington: University Press of Kentucky, 2014.

Piehler, G. Kurt, and Sidney Pash, eds. *The United States and the Second World War: New Perspectives on Diplomacy, War, and the Home Front*. New York: Fordham University Press, 2010.

Rees, David. *Harry Dexter White: A Study in Paradox*. New York: Coward, McCann & Geoghegan, 1973.

Robinson, Greg. *By Order of the President: FDR and the Internment of Japanese Americans*. Cambridge: Harvard University Press, 2001.

Sayre, Francis B. *Glad Adventure*. New York, Macmillan, 1957.

Schroeder, Paul W. *The Axis Alliance and Japanese-American Relations 1941*. Ithaca: Cornell University Press, 1958.

Schwarz, Jordan A. *The Speculator*. Chapel Hill: University of North Carolina Press, 1981.

Shigemitsu, Mamoru. *Japan and Her Destiny*. New York: Dutton, 1956.

Sloan, Bill. *Given Up for Dead: America's Heroic Stand at Wake Island*. New York: Bantam, 2008.

Smith, Richard Norton. *Uncommon Man: The Triumph of Herbert Hoover*. New York: Simon & Schuster, 1985.

Stevenson, William. *A Man Called Intrepid*. New York: Harcourt Brace Jovanovich, 1976.

Sturbrock, Donald. *Storyteller: The Authorized Biography of Roald Dahl*. New York: Simon & Schuster, 2010.

Sugihara, Seishiro. *Between Incompetence and Culpability: Assessing the Diplomacy of Japan's Foreign Ministry from Pearl Harbor to Potsdam*. Lanham, MD: University Press of America, 1997.

Swann Sebastian. *Japan's Imperial Dilemma in China: The Tientsin Incident, 1939-1940*. London: Routledge, 2012.

Takeda, T. *Kan'ichi Asakawa: A Historian Who Worked for World Peace*. Tokyo: Taiyo, 2007.

Terasaki, Gwen, *Bridge to the Sun*. Chapel Hill: University of North Carolina Press, 1957.

Thorne, Christopher. *The Issue of War*. New York: Oxford University Press, 1985.

Togo, Shigenori. *The Cause of Japan*. New York: Simon & Schuster, 1956.

Toland, John. *The Rising Sun: The Decline and Fall of the Japanese Empire, 1936-1945*. New York: Random House, 1970.

Tollischus, Otto D. *Tokyo Record*. New York: Reynal and Hitchcock, 1943.

Trotter, Ann. *Britain and East Asia, 1933-1937*. Cambridge, UK: Cambridge University Press, 1975.

Tully, Grace. *FDR, My Boss*. New York: Scribner's, 1949.

US Congress. *Hearings Before the Joint Committee on the Investigation of the Pearl Harbor Attack*. Washington, DC: US Government Printing Office, 1946.

US Department of Defense. *The "Magic" Background of Pearl Harbor*. 8 vols. Washington, DC: US Government Printing Office, 1978.

US Department of State. *Foreign Relations of the United States: Japan, 1931-1941*. 2 vols. Washington, DC: US Government Printing Office, 1943.

US Department of State. *Foreign Relations of the United States, 1941*. Washington, DC: US Government Printing Office, 1956.

Utley, Jonathan G. *Going to War With Japan, 1937*-1941. Knoxville: University of Tennessee Press, 1985.

Watanabe, Yoji. *Rikugun jikken sentoukitai* (Army Experimental Fighter Squadrons). Tokyo: Green Arrow, 1999.

Watt, David Cameron. *How War Came*. New York: Pantheon, 1989.

Welles, Sumner. *Time for Decision*. New York: Harper, 1944.

White, Ashley. Saburo Kurusu Euro Project. http://www.youtube.com/watch?v=khThOQkh3Sw.

Wohlstetter, Roberta. *Pearl Harbor: Warning and Decision*. Stanford, CA: Stanford University Press, 1962.

Zacharias, Ellis M. *Secret Missions*. New York: Putnam's, 1946.

Archives and Personal Papers

Borthwick Historical Institute, York, UK: Lord Halifax Diaries.

Franklin D. Roosevelt Library, Hyde Park, NY: Adolf Berle MSS, Francis Biddle MSS, Betty Hite MSS, Mrs. Charles Hamlin MSS, Henry Morgenthau Jr. MSS, Eleanor Roosevelt MSS, Franklin D. Roosevelt MSS, John Toland MSS, Rexford Tugwell MSS, Sumner Welles MSS, and Claude Wickard Diaries.

Great Britain, Public Record Office, Kew, UK: Foreign Office Records: FO/371, United States.

Herbert Hoover Presidential Library, West Branch, IA: William R. Castle MSS, Herbert Hoover MSS, and Ferdinand Mayer MSS.

Houghton Library, Harvard University, Cambridge, MA: William R. Castle Jr. Diaries, Joseph Grew MSS, J. Pierrepont Moffat MSS, and Robert E. Sherwood MSS.

Library of Congress, Washington, DC: Joseph E. Davies MSS, Courtney Letts de Espil MSS, Herbert Feis MSS, Cordell Hull MSS, Harold Ickes MSS, Breckinridge Long MSS, Francis B. Sayre MSS, and Huston Thompson MSS.

National Diet Library, Tokyo: Saburo Kurusu MSS.

Seeley Mudd Library, Princeton University, Princeton, NJ: Bernard M. Baruch MSS, Arthur Krock MSS, and Harry Dexter White MSS.

Sterling Library, Yale University, New Haven, CT: Kan'ichi Asakawa MSS and Henry L. Stimson MSS.

US National Archives, Washington, DC: US State Department records, Record Group 59.

Index

About the Editors

Carol K. Davidge

J. GARRY CLIFFORD was an award-winning historian and the author or editor of numerous books, including *Presidents, Diplomats, and Other Mortals*, with Theodore A. Wilson (University of Missouri Press).

MASAKO R. OKURA is Associate Professor of Political Science and Public Administration at Columbus State University in Columbus, Georgia.